Reignition

TRANSFORMING

STUCK STARTUPS INTO

BREAKOUT WINNERS

Reignition

DAVE HERSH

AN INC.
ORIGINAL

An Inc. Original
New York, New York
www.anincoriginal.com

Distributed by Greenleaf Book Group

For ordering information or special discounts for bulk purchases, please contact Greenleaf Book Group at PO Box 91869, Austin, TX 78709, 512.891.6100.

Design and composition by Greenleaf Book Group
Cover design by Greenleaf Book Group
Cover images used under license from ©Adobestock.com

Publisher's Cataloging-in-Publication data is available.

Print ISBN: 978-1-63909-034-1

eBook ISBN: 978-1-63909-035-8

To offset the number of trees consumed in the printing of our books, Greenleaf donates a portion of the proceeds from each printing to the Arbor Day Foundation. Greenleaf Book Group has replaced over 50,000 trees since 2007.

Printed in the United States of America on acid-free paper

24 25 26 27 28 29 30 31   10 9 8 7 6 5 4 3 2 1

First Edition

For April, Matt and Hazel

Contents

It Sucks to Be Stuck

It's hard enough leading a startup. But it's even worse when the company's outlook is bleak, options are limited, and everyone is looking at you desperately, hoping you have the magic bullet that will save you all.

It sucks to be stuck.

As I write this, the economy is finally suffering a recession after 13 years of massive investment and expansion. Startup leaders are struggling to find financing, running layoffs, shifting strategies on the fly, selling themselves for pennies on the dollar, and feeling the weight of failure.

The previous downturn, the worst recession since World War II, began in 2007. The startup I helped found six years earlier and was running at the time, Jive, had bootstrapped its way through the rough gauntlet of entrepreneurship to achieve a healthy, profitable $12 million business selling software to companies that wanted more innovative ways of communicating with employees, customers, partners, and fans. People loved our software, and we were the best at what we did.

When Facebook came on the scene around 2006, we saw a huge opportunity to bring the technology and experience behind social networking to large companies to improve how their employees collaborated. Desperate to expand and win this new market, we raised $15 million in late 2007 from a top venture capital (VC) firm. But like many young companies who raise venture, we tried to force growth, hired the wrong people, kept the wrong management team in place, and ran the wrong strategy. In 2008 we dramatically missed our sales goal two quarters in a row. Then in September, several large, formerly unshakeable investment banks collapsed from the subprime mortgage crisis. Jive was draining money, the world was collapsing, and the newly established board was threatening my CEO job.

I felt alone and unqualified—a fraud. We had built a healthy, sustainable business, but the minute we tried to fuel faster growth using the traditional VC playbook, things went sideways. Now we were stuck, and it was on my shoulders to fix it or be pushed aside. And there wasn't a great playbook for that.

Since my time at Jive, and as a consultant, product leader, CFO, founder, CEO, venture capitalist, private equity investor, strategic advisor, board member, CEO coach, advisor, and executive chairman, I have seen hundreds of companies and startup leaders in similar situations. I have taken a company public, acquired many others, and failed too many times to count—but I also succeeded enough times to keep playing the game and loving it.

After a couple of decades, one ugly and consistent theme has always bothered me about the startup journey: the waste.

Vast amounts of time, energy, and money—not to mention the hopes and dreams of the people involved—are squandered in pursuit of unrealistic growth and milestones.

What do I mean by stuck? It means that you've run out of options. You may be out of cash, still have some runway, or even be profitable, but you can't find a growth path that aligns with your investors and/or aspirations. The business isn't living up to its vision, and employees, investors, board members, and executives are feeling the pain. The business is swirling around an eddy instead of flowing down the river to its ideal destination.

In my experience, getting stuck is rarely the product of a down economy but more often the product of an inefficient system. The path of fundraising and hypergrowth is designed for an elite subset of companies that make it through the gauntlet of large-market dominance. Unfortunately, most companies don't make it and get stuck in some capacity, where options for getting out are limited. And while this book is not intended only for companies that raised money (bootstrapped companies get stuck too), I want to start with the inherent problems in the fundraising system.

A System That Promotes Failure

Raising VC has an air of "making it" for many founders. The media fuels this thinking with handpicked stories of successful fundraising, initial public offerings (IPOs), big acquisitions, and unicorns that make the process sound easy. It's also promoted in startup circles where founders measure their funding against their peers as a proxy for success. Add to this the pressure of competitors raising money, overly optimistic strategies and operating plans, the relief of having a healthy balance sheet, and a belief that raising money signals success in the market.

This thinking has become pervasive for entrepreneurs, especially in the major tech startup areas like San Francisco, Austin, and New York. So much so that entrepreneurs use fundraising rounds as a lazy shorthand for indicating where their company is in its trajectory: "We're a Series B company building toward our Series C metrics so we can raise early next year." Instead of seeing funding rounds as enabling business strategy, they're using them as the basis for setting company goals.

This tail-wagging-the-dog problem leads thousands of high-potential companies to get stuck every year. Why? Because the odds of success are very low. The VC model is essentially, "Grow fast or get out of the way." Startups do anything in their power to maintain high growth, but it's incredibly challenging. So most companies die a painful death trying to grow too fast as the money runs dry and the business is forced to sell at a loss. This happens at least 77 percent of the time in VC-backed companies.[1]

And this system keeps getting bigger. In 1980, 30 VC firms were managing $3 billion. Today, about 2,000 firms manage roughly $600 billion. When I started my professional life in 1995, during a healthy economy, there was $8 billion invested

---

1   "Venture Capital Funnel Shows Odds of Becoming a Unicorn Are about 1%," cbinsights.com, September 6, 2018, https://www.cbinsights.com/research/venture-capital-funnel-2/.

annually; in 2021 (a record year), it was $345 billion. 2022 returned to earth somewhat at $241 billion of investment,[2] but despite the downturn, companies are still raising large amounts of money, and I wouldn't expect the odds of startup success to become more favorable.

So how does an industry with such a low success rate become such a huge part of the infrastructure? VC is a "hits business." VC funds make their returns on roughly one out of ten investments doing incredibly well (above a 5X return). The huge winners generate the profits. That's fine for the firms and the winners, but what about the other companies? Trillions of dollars in value, not to mention the happiness of startup leaders, employees, and customers, are destroyed because of a misalignment between the expectations of invested capital and startups' ability to execute.

Some of these companies just didn't work. They failed to get traction and were liquidated. Somewhere between 25 to 40 percent of investments return no capital, according to the National Venture Capital Association (NVCA),[3] which doesn't necessarily mean those companies are complete failures, but it does give you a sense of that end-of-the-success curve. There are a lot of reasons why these companies fail, but the important point is that they can't be saved.

2   National Venture Capital Association, NVCA Yearbook, 26th ed., 2023. https://nvca.org/nvca-yearbook/.

3   Deborah Gage, "The Venture Capital Secret: 3 Out of 4 Start-Ups Fail," *Wall Street Journal*, September 20, 2012, https://www.wsj.com/articles/SB1000087239639044 37202045780049804776429190.

In between the winners and failures, however, are companies that get the short end of the stick: teams with great potential that go too fast and exhaust their runway before they figure out the ideal business model. These teams invest years of blood, sweat, and tears in building a startup and don't get the benefits of a broad portfolio. If they don't grow quickly enough, they are sold off or shut down to make room for the next. This abandoned cohort—companies with beloved products and actual revenue that need more time to hone their strategy—is where I have spent much of my time.

MIDDLE-DISTANCE STARTUPS

There are three types of running events in track: short distance, middle distance, and long distance. Short distance is characterized by explosive acceleration and maintaining top speed throughout the race. Long distance is mostly about consistent endurance and sustainability. But middle-distance events like the 400m, 800m, or 1,600m are the most strategic of the races. Runners must constantly monitor their position, energy, and the race stage and decide when to surge and when to draft. Great middle-distance runners have speed, agility, endurance . . . and cunning.

Many stuck companies I work with are like middle-distance runners forced to run as if in a short-distance event. When they should be preserving energy and drafting behind other companies as they figure out the right time to strike, they instead burst out of the gates with everything they have, destroying their energy and oxygen such that they can't finish the race. Their potential is shattered before they figure out the right model.

If you feel that maybe you ran too fast in the wrong direction—that you have the makings of a powerful company inside your startup but can't seem to get on the path—this book is for you. Getting unstuck is possible. You can define your success and eliminate the dangers of competing in a game with few winners. I wrote this book to show you how.

A Different Way to Play the Game

At first, I saw this structural inefficiency as an opportunity. I devised a contrarian strategy for transforming slower-growth startups into healthy, sustainable, purposeful, and profitable companies. Initially, I did this as a consultant and advisor. Eventually, I started acquiring stuck companies to reinvigorate them through focus and execution. Once healthy, I would look for breakout growth opportunities or merging with other companies, but I wouldn't force either of those paths. My philosophy was (and continues to be): if we build a great company, we will have options. I later partnered with another former founder and CEO to acquire larger companies.

The work has been challenging but satisfying. I have had the chance to work with great people and roll up my sleeves on challenging projects. I love what I do. And yet, I quickly realized I wasn't making a meaningful impact on the systemic waste problem.

I can only work on a few startups at a time, but I want

to help many more companies with great products, cultures, and visions that have gotten stuck. I want to share what I've learned about startup turnaround. If I can give those companies another "bite at the apple" to build something great, perhaps I can make the lives of those who lead them better while nibbling away at the cancerous wake of destruction caused by premature scaling.

Reignition: Transforming Stuck Startups into Breakout Winners was the answer.

ABOUT THE BOOK

I wrote this book first and foremost for startups and growth companies, from $1 million to $100 million in revenue, that have had some success—just not as much of it as investors expected—and now need to consider transforming the business in order to survive. Second, I also intended it to help founders and leaders of bootstrapped, healthy, or earlier-stage startups see the minefields ahead to avoid common mistakes around premature scaling. Third, I want this book to serve as a playbook for companies acquiring stuck companies or new "hired" leaders coming into companies to get them healthy. And finally, I hope that investors and stakeholders can learn new strategies for helping leaders through challenging times. My goal is to expose readers to a different path that could be much more valuable and rewarding in the long run.

Getting unstuck is possible. I can show you how.

In this book, I'll show you that you don't have to play this constant-funding-as-the-only-means-to-win game. You can rebuild a meaningful entity where the investment capital is the gas in the tank, not the driver of the car; where the customer needs reign, not quarterly numbers; and where, most importantly, you can get unstuck and enjoy the ride.

This book is not about raising capital versus bootstrapping. I'm not against VC or private equity (PE), which are essential to the startup ecosystem. Companies need capital to fuel growth and help from smart, connected people, and VC is often the best means to build great companies. The issue is not always *whether* VC but *how much* and *when*.

Put simply, staying lean, disciplined, and focused on your core business can buy you the time and space you need to optimize your company's long-term trajectory. Instead of spreading yourself too thin strategically, which usually leads to getting stuck, you focus on a smaller product and market strategy you can dominate. Instead of expanding too quickly beyond your winnable niche, you focus on that niche and let the pull of the market drive your expansion. Knowing your "core"—what you are or can be the best in the world at doing—is the key to building a great company, but it's also the key to getting unstuck. It's the essence of transformation.

FIRST CHANGE YOURSELF

Another significant—and rarely discussed—element of getting unstuck is how we show up as leaders. A deep dive into our mindset, blind spots, motivations, and how our team perceives us is perhaps the most challenging but essential part of the transformation process. And I want to call it out early.

Why? Because many of the reasons companies get stuck are the result of the mindset we bring to decisions. Instead of serving customers, we subconsciously serve our own needs without notice. Years of hard work can be destroyed by something we don't see happening.

For example, my blind spot is a hero complex that drives me to rescue people and companies. This means I am emotionally attached to "doing well by my colleagues" and often stay in businesses long after I should have moved on. If I don't constantly check myself on that mindset, everyone suffers the pain of failure because the process is dragged out.

Ensuring you can be the leader your company needs during a transformation requires an honest inventory of what holds you back and how to overcome those obstacles to build a robust and independent business. Ultimately, our companies won't change unless we do. We must unpack our mindset before the restructuring work can begin. Otherwise, the patterns will repeat themselves.

THE STAGES OF TRANSFORMATION

After thoroughly analyzing how you got stuck and the mindsets that drove decision-making, you can get started on the company's transformation.

First, you must restructure your company around your "best-in-the-world" core strength. When, and only when, the company is healthy can you thoughtfully experiment with expansion possibilities. Once you discover the right growth path, you can intelligently decide how to finance the company and be "reborn" to the market with powerful positioning.

Here is a breakdown of each stage of transformation, each of which is a chapter in the book.

1. **Assess what happened:** Do an honest inventory of how you got stuck. Review the typical symptoms of stuck companies and diagnose your missteps. Then answer the difficult question: "Does it make sense to keep going?" This is your starting point for transformation. Not every company is worth saving, so an honest assessment is essential.

2. **Become the leader your company needs now:** Your company won't transform until you do. What were your motivations, and how did they lead to your situation? Unless you work through your blind spots, you'll repeat history.

3. **Get focused:** Identify what you are the best in the world at doing that customers crave—your "core"—and build a lean, focused team around that strength. Instead of focusing on growth, focus on winning a smaller market beyond a shadow of a doubt and creating a healthy business to give yourself time and space to figure out your breakout opportunity.

4. **Focus your team:** The path to getting healthy requires a new way of conducting business: realistic goals, strong culture, effective operations, and streamlined, inclusive

communication. The output of this phase is a business that is in "fighting shape"—lean, disciplined, and single-minded in its pursuit of a new mission.

5. **Evaluate growth thoughtfully:** When the business is healthy and (possibly even) profitable, you have "earned the right" to run growth experiments. This process of learning and discovery requires patience. But, if done well, you'll find growth opportunities that build from your core while carving out a larger and ripe market space you can win.

6. **Scale intelligently:** It's time to build a robust, data-driven growth plan based on actual results and customer "pull." This will clarify the market opportunity and help you find the right investment partner.

7. **Tell your new story:** When your growth path is clear, and you've got the right financing to support it, execution comes down to excellent leadership, culture, management, and storytelling. Design a positioning and accompanying narrative that builds from your core to inspire customers and motivate employees while opening up new market space.

At the end of each chapter, I have included a section called "Hard Lessons," which consists of stories from my own career of how I have made poor decisions and learned from them. Hopefully my mistakes can help you avoid your own.

I have used this process many times to help companies get

unstuck. While the progression of steps roughly models the sequential arc of transformation and the order in which things typically should happen, the reality is often more nuanced. Some stages will overlap with others, and the steps may occur at different times or, in some cases, become an ongoing activity for your team.

Ripping Off the Band-Aid

Back in 2008, as a young CEO at Jive facing a stuck company and a shattered economy, I had no choice but to act. We had gotten stuck because I had followed investors' playbook advice and tried to grow too fast in the wrong direction with the wrong people. I was scared and angry, but also driven to rebuild. I cut 66 people—a third of the company—and hired an experienced executive team to support a new mission and plan for profitable growth. In a spur-of-the-moment decision, I even told the company that if we hit our goal that quarter, I would get a tattoo of the number 8 (for $8 million in new revenue).

What happened next shocked me. Instead of feeling overwhelmed by having fewer people, we produced more, enjoyed the work, collaborated well, hit our goals, and put cash back into the business. The company felt like a boxer who had shed weight to crush it in the ideal weight class. We were lean, driven, purposeful, and in a focused flow state, doing what we did well. We doubled sales and put cash back into the business. The company grew into the leader of the category we helped create and, ultimately, became a public company. We became one of the hottest companies in tech (until things went sideways again, but that's another story). All because we were able to do the hard work of transformation.

I have seen this pattern too many times to count. With too much money and hubris, we got lazy and overly ambitious, spreading ourselves thin on top of an infrastructure that wasn't ready for that level of growth. When we were disciplined, connected as a team, and focused, we were pulled into the right market opportunities, and greatness happened.

Since then, I have honed the ideas in this book, not just for companies that need a turnaround but for any company that seeks longevity and strength.

I'm not alone in this realization. Many founders I've met have told me they had to kill a company before they understood what overcapitalizing and scaling prematurely look like. Almost always, these founders approach company building more patiently and austerely the next time. Only through experience is the playbook seen for the damage it can wreak. Attempting to grow at all costs—trying to shortcut the path to success—almost always fails. Even if there is some financial outcome, these leaders later regret their approach and the missed opportunity to build their company the right way.

The most profound gains in value I have witnessed came during periods of austerity (and often global economic uncertainty). If you can get past the need for overly fast gains and learn to be a middle-distance startup with agility, strength, resolve, and strategic might, you will give yourself the best shot at greatness.

I have made many of the mistakes I review in this book and probably wasted billions in value because I succumbed to those same forces of hubristic fundraising, scaling, and mis-hiring. But it gives me pleasure and purpose to share with you these mistakes (alongside some victories) and stories from successful founders and CEOs. If your business is worth saving, I'll give you the roadmap. Executed with commitment, discipline, and grit, this path will expose enormous opportunities for wealth creation but, more importantly, for meaning and becoming your best leader.

Transformation doesn't come easily. Nor is it merely a financial equation. The outcome will be better than you imagine—and certainly better than staying on the current path. As George Eliot said, "It's never too late to be what you might have been." I'm as sure of that as the number 8 tattoo on my ankle.

CHAPTER 1

Assess What Happened– What Went Wrong? Is It Fixable?

Where you stumble and fall, there you will find gold.

—JOSEPH CAMPBELL

"I t's not working, Adam. We're going to bring in a professional CEO."

Adam couldn't believe it. How had it gotten to this point, he wondered. How could the investors he had brought on to help him now be pushing him out? What went wrong? Things had been going so well.

Adam Schoenfeld and two bright, visionary entrepreneurs founded Simply Measured in 2010. Like most founders, they didn't set out to build a billion-dollar juggernaut. They wanted to solve a problem, create something great together, and maybe make money and enjoy the process. At first, the company didn't even have an idea, much less a product. But they were familiar with a growing trend: social media marketing. Marketers were flooding channels like Twitter and Facebook (now Meta) to find new customers. However, because it was new, those marketers couldn't measure the impact of their efforts.

Being spreadsheet-savvy data geeks, Adam and the team focused on surfacing data to help these marketers make better decisions. Their first product was a simple spreadsheet that tracked tweets for companies. Customers loved it. And they started paying for it. By the end of the first year, Simply Measured had $50,000 in monthly revenue. The co-founders raised $750,000 (note: I was an investor) to add a few more employees and fuel growth. With five productive sales reps, the startup was a well-oiled machine, and the business was thriving.

That's when VC firms came knocking. It was time to "put gas in the engine," they told him. Adam was initially reluctant, as Simply Measured had a good thing going. But with the encouragement of his team and friends, he started to believe he could turn this simple product into a billion-dollar company.

In 2012 they raised $8 million. That allowed him and his co-founders to grow their team and expand on their core offering, which at that point, was an advanced version of the spreadsheet Adam had built two years earlier. The social media analytics market was growing fast, but for Simply Measured to sustain the growth investors wanted, they would have to move into a larger market. The company was what investors call "TAM-constrained," that is, its total available market (TAM) was too small to achieve the needed growth. The founders were forced to take their company into the larger, uncharted territory of marketing analytics.

While there were many potential buyers with money in this new market, it was full of well-funded competitors. And Simply Measured's core offering was not robust or unique enough for the market's needs. Still, investors were bullish, and Adam and the team were ambitious. In 2014, they raised another $20 million to expand their offering, grow revenue, and become a dominant player.

Then things started to stumble.

With five sales reps, they were productive; but now with twenty, things got messy. There weren't enough opportunities, so the salespeople couldn't make quota and got frustrated. Smaller startups were filling the market gaps, while Simply Measured was no longer agile enough to adapt to the latest trends.

"We were forcing growth with an unproven product in an unfamiliar market," Adam told me. "And we made it worse by hiring execs who didn't understand our offering, opportunity, or culture." By 2015 the growth rate had slowed and no longer met investor expectations. Adam was forced out.

The board wanted more financial discipline, so they hired an operations-focused CEO. Innovation took a backseat to financial metrics to get the company back on track. But with the market changing rapidly, that strategy failed to get the company healthy enough to survive. Customers were finding other vendors with more modern offerings that matched the rapidly changing landscape of marketing channels. The business never recovered and was sold a few years later in a transaction far below expectations.

"I was young and naïve," Adam shared. "There was never a discussion about *not* raising money, only about when and how much. If we had only raised $2 million or $3 million, we would have had a great outcome for everyone. Instead, we spent time figuring out how to build a billion-dollar company and couldn't see what was happening in front of us."

Adam went on to start more companies, either by bootstrapping or by being disciplined around only raising as much as he knew he could put to work effectively. After suffering the pain of premature growth with Simply Measured, he routinely asked himself the following questions: Does the strategy feel ambitious but achievable? Am I doing the right thing for my customers, or have I lost touch with their needs? Am I doing it *my* way—or am I running someone else's playbook?

Understanding Why You Got Stuck

Adam's story is sadly common. A startup finds early traction in a niche market and uses that traction to justify taking on a larger, more crowded market before its offering and team are ready. The founders raise too much, scale prematurely, lose focus, waste time and money, and burn out their team. Problems that seem like typical growing pains or isolated issues—frustrated sales reps, high customer acquisition costs (CACs), rapidly shifting priorities—are the canary in the coal mine of the company's demise.

"Scaling prematurely" is the primary existential challenge faced by startups and growth companies. It's easy to diagnose in hindsight but hard to see when you're in the fog of war, surrounded by a hypergrowth-obsessed culture and anxious investors. The desire to win (or survive) drives impatient decision-making around scant data points, which snowballs into a flailing, overweight organizational structure that burns through cash while not hitting its goals. Before we can see the error of our ways, we get stuck: no more money, no more growth, and no more options.

The first step to getting unstuck is understanding how you got stuck, regardless of your situation. How did you get to this point? What decisions got you here? How did you justify those decisions? What data did you miss or ignore? Incorporate as many perspectives as possible—primarily your team's, but also investors', customers', and other stakeholders'—to get a complete picture.

Once you've reflected on your past challenges, you must answer the most challenging question of all: Should you keep going? If there is a potentially promising future, the rest of the book will guide the way. If not, you can apply the practical advice you learn here to your next venture so you don't make the same mistakes twice.

What's Your Problem?

In my experience, getting stuck manifests in five primary ways: hiring the wrong team, fixating on revenue over strategy, losing focus, buying into a distorted narrative, or failing to manage through disruptive shifts. To help you diagnose which problems led to your stalled state, let's look at these issues and their symptoms.

PROBLEM 1: HIRING THE WRONG TEAM

Growing a startup requires different skills than getting it off the ground. You need the right talent at the right time to handle the distinct needs of your startup at various stages of its lifecycle.

An easy way to think about a startup's lifecycle is in four main stages: (1) find your "thing," (2) build a business, (3) scale the business, and (4) run it profitably. When you are in the thick of running a new business, it's not always clear what stage you're in, but it's obvious in hindsight as you reflect on how the story unfolded. Here is a breakdown of the right talent needed for each stage:

Unfortunately, startups often hire the wrong talent for the stage they are in. Here are some common hiring fails:

- **Hiring the wrong people:** Early-stage startup leaders (me included) often hire later-stage talent before those skills are needed. For example, Stage 3 employees at a Stage 1 company will need more management and structure

	Stage 1 Find your "thing"	Stage 2 Build a business	Stage 3 Scale the business	Stage 4 Run it profitably
Objective	Test and experiment with your offering; work through the kinks; and find the right product/market fit, even if it's aimed at only a small segment of the market initially.	Grow revenue while fine-tuning the business model (sales, channel, markets, product) that will drive differentiation, scale, and repeatability.	Hone the long-term infrastructure for growth (e.g., systems, processes, people) based on market pull, sustainable differentiation, and a clear opportunity at a larger market.	Streamline the company for profitable, sustainable performance and protection of core markets while carefully exploring expansion paths.
Talent	**Creators**: Broad-thinking, creative, flexible, mission-driven, product and market pros who can bring a new entity to life.	**Builders**: Scrappy, collaborative business-builders who are flexible yet strategic and can test and build systems, teams, and processes.	**Scalers**: Experienced executives and employees with deep skills and the agility to handle market shifts.	**Maintainers**: Experienced professionals who can hone systems and processes for efficiency and customer value.

Figure 1.1 Company Stages

than is feasible for a small team. They don't often have the flexible do-what-it-takes mindset or experience necessary to bring order out of chaos. Later-stage execs will also attempt to build out the machinery of scale too early while the business is still forming. This is akin to adding doors and tires before knowing whether you are assembling a helicopter, truck, or lawn mower.

- **Hiring too many people:** When founders raise money, they often think about the time in which they must *spend* that money—for example, "18 months of runway"—and manage to that arbitrary destination. They often hire people based on the most optimistic operating budget, giving them a feeling of success as they check the box on a new hire. But this approach shortens the runway and adds more communication "nodes" to an employee network that needs to operate nimbly as it finds its way in the market. This is like in the movies when the hero is trying to defuse a bomb, and he or she inevitably cuts a wire that makes the countdown timer go faster. Every hire you make shortens your "fuse" and adds to the stress.

- **Hiring "B players":** Startup founders typically have a core strength, like product design or marketing. That focus may lead them to bring on a world-class team in their department but fail to hire at the same level across other parts of the business. For example, a product founder might hire a later-stage sales leader who is capable and steady but unsuitable for an early-stage company. The founder wants someone to "take care of sales while we do the important product work." The sales leader then focuses on scaling her team quickly with other B players, and the organization becomes confused and stressed and burns too much cash.

- **Keeping people for too long:** Startup leaders tend to keep people in positions long after their abilities have capped out. While loyalty is admirable, it's useless if it leads to a stalled venture. If a company has progressed to Stages 2 or 3 but is still operating with a Stage 1 team to manage this larger company, that team may lack the experience to orchestrate smart growth. This problem is not only seen through all the stages but can also happen in the *opposite* direction. For example, if a new technology disrupts an industry, a company may need to return to Stage 1 and assemble the talent to reinvent its offering. Or if a company hired people expecting growth that never materialized, it might need to downsize for financial viability. Executives will need to be replaced by, or augmented with, people who can support the needs of that stage.

In my experience, nothing is more impactful to the business than having the right team at the right time. And leaner is always better, in my opinion. The right team with the right mission will figure out markets, products, and channels and weather the storm of uncertainty, misfortune, and stress. This is not a perfect science and often comes down to your leadership intuition on how that team is comprised—are you convinced you have the right team with the right marching orders? Here are three warning signs that you've hired the wrong team:

- **Warning sign #1: Low employee morale.** When people aren't a good fit for your startup's current stage and goals are missed, employees become frustrated. It's hard for them to put energy into something when they don't understand their job or priorities or see the results of their efforts. And if you have a lot of new employees along with first-time managers, your HR problems can spiral out of control. When HR problems arise, leaders often try to resolve them with cultural "Band-Aids" like free meals or foosball tables. But nothing replaces the need to experience mutual success. Culture is best when people feel a sense of belonging to a high-performing organization—when they love their team, are getting stuff done, *and* the company is winning. Culture sucks if the company isn't winning.

- *Metrics to Watch*: increased turnover, declining employee satisfaction

- **Warning sign #2: You hire more but produce less.** You build a larger team in pursuit of new markets, but the results don't scale. The dollars you invest in new roles don't match the growth numbers on your spreadsheets. This requires a deep analysis of current and forward-looking data to determine whether your team is working as expected, as it may take time for new hires to "ramp" toward full productivity. Less-experienced executives can be misled by fancy slides that indicate new hires are making progress but mask core problems.

  - *Metrics to Watch*: decreased revenue or profit per employee or department, declining operating productivity (for your industry), increasing overhead costs to sales ratio, lower percent of milestones or objective and key results (OKRs) achieved

- **Warning sign #3: Your leadership team is confused about priorities.** Do your execs exude confidence and excitement, or do they have a "deer in the headlights" look that betrays their uncertainty and confusion? Are they coming to you with problems because they don't know what to do or coming to you with well-analyzed solutions? If employees are seething under the surface rather than working through conflict professionally, or their updates aren't crisp, concise, and aligned with the company's goals, you may have the wrong team for your stage—or the reality of the company's situation may not match the story. The tone of your executives is a significant indicator of how your overall team is doing. Make sure you're tuned into it.

  - *Metrics to Watch*: declining board satisfaction and performance reviews; the amount of one-on-one meeting time your execs spend on "finger pointing" or needing help with decisions; percent of company OKRs or key metrics achieved

Analyze your team's performance carefully with an eye open to these warning signs. But don't ignore your gut: What does your intuition say about your current team? The most effective startups are comprised of a lean group of passionate people driven to deliver on a larger scale. When people are pushed a bit beyond their experience and are focused but not overly stressed, companies achieve a "flow state" where the results are strong, and the people are excited. How far or close is your team to this ideal?

PROBLEM 2: FIXATING ON REVENUE OVER STRATEGY

No single metric has more drama surrounding it than quarterly revenue. Make it, and you're a hero. Miss it, and you're out of a job. But fixating on it kills companies.

There's nothing wrong with having a quarterly target: Cash is the oxygen of a growth business and needs to be managed carefully. But the true strategic priorities of your startup—learning, balancing innovation with growth, finding great customers, hiring the right people—are often lost on board members who only spend a small amount of time with you. So quarterly metrics become shorthand for success. Because your board is your boss, they push down pressure to make quarterly revenues in ways that lead to destructive decisions and disguise the real issues faced by the company.

If your startup is still learning to navigate its market, you *must* reduce the pressure for revenue in favor of a deep, unwavering focus on long-term health. When you don't, your sales team (and sometimes the whole company) may respond to this monthly or quarterly pressure with a do-whatever-it-takes mentality leading to chaos in the name of bringing in more revenue. The result? You push innovation aside, compromise market positioning, turn your product into a dumpster of features, and create a trail of mayhem trying to keep customers happy. And every subsequent quarter becomes increasingly trickier.

A friend refers to this problem as "playing house": Board meetings are conducted as if the company were a huge public company, but it is still figuring out product/market fit. The CEO focuses on discreet marketing and sales metrics before the business model is even close to being baked. This is a form of theater that is strangely common, especially when a CEO who wants to look professional is coupled with a board that isn't deep enough into the business.

To understand the extent to which focusing on short-term results is affecting or even stalling your business, answer these questions: How are you treating your sales goals? Do they accurately reflect where you are as a business? Or is the pressure to meet unrealistic growth rates stressing your team and hurting innovation?

Here are three warning signs you are overly fixating on revenue:

- **Warning sign #1: Not hitting your growth goal.** Investors attach an assumed growth rate to your startup based on industry benchmarks. If you fail to hit your numbers, you may have an arbitrary growth goal that doesn't reflect your market dynamics or stage in the startup's lifecycle. Ideally, you communicate reasonable financial goals alongside ambitious strategic goals to your investors.

  - *Metrics to Watch*: declining quarterly growth rate,

lower sales productivity by customer type, lower profit per customer, lower revenue or earnings per share

- **Warning sign #2: Unclear strategy.** If employees don't understand what's important or the plan to achieve those goals, they can't make intelligent decisions. When revenue goals are the only visible metric, employees make decisions that look good in the short term but can kill the company over the long haul.

  - *Metrics to Watch*: OKR attainment, win rate in core markets, misaligned goals across different teams

- **Warning sign #3: Frustrated product team.** A heavy focus on revenue goals will burden the product team the most. Why? A sales-focused CEO will whipsaw the product organization by constantly focusing on every hot new opportunity. Good products have well-thought-out roadmaps that only shift when it's clearly the right thing for the company. Constant changes will wear out the team and cause good players to leave and innovation to slow.

  - *Metrics to Watch*: OKR attainment, roadmap achievement, product team satisfaction, win rate in core markets

You may be intent on tripling your business in a year because that will allow you to raise more capital, but keeping an eye out for these warning signs and corresponding metrics will let you know if your goals are realistic. It might be better to only grow 50 percent this year on a leaner team, learn more about your market, build more products, and double your size the following year.

The most significant value creation comes when companies set the right strategic goals while staying lean in pursuing those goals. Their founders and leadership team tell their board, "We'll keep costs down and extend our runway if you help us focus on these priorities that will drive long-term health and scale." Those execs don't focus on "easy" metrics like revenue but rather set strategically important and concrete goals (e.g., "10 customers in our target vertical with 300 percent first-year ROI and an overall NPS score over 50.").

PROBLEM 3: LOSING FOCUS

I hear alarm bells when I hear founders make statements like, "We have a consumer product and a business product;" "We are expanding to four new vertical markets this year;" and "We're going to light up our reseller channel now." These suggest a lack of focus and often portend the beginning of getting stuck.

Staying true to your core—the one thing you do well—is tricky when you feel the pressure to grow. Having controlled experiments to test new markets and features is fine. But often, startups confuse experiments with execution and future expansion opportunities with their core business. I've been involved in many whiteboard sessions where market categories are casually illustrated like pellets for Pac-Man to consume. Instead of running thoughtful experiments to test whether and how to compete in those markets—and assemble the best offering for them—the leadership team shifts expensive human resources toward trying to conquer the markets out of the gate.

Your team will naturally want to follow you into new, exciting territory, so you must be deliberate about where you focus. Great businesses are built by doing *one* thing exceedingly well and ensuring that success is clear and measurable. Fail to focus your business, and you will run into the following problems:

- **Conflicting priorities:** Your team can't make good decisions.

- **Board confusion:** Your board is ineffective at helping your company grow and expects too much growth too early.

- **Unrealistic company goals:** The ambitions of your operating plans outpace your team's ability to execute, slowly killing their motivation.

- **Dwindling cash:** You run out of money before you figure out the right path.

- **Customer dissatisfaction:** Customers grow sour on your increasingly diluted offering.

- **Sluggish reaction to market:** You can't innovate quickly, and competitors win market share.

- **Diluted product:** Your product team gets confused and frustrated about what to build.

- **Murky story:** Your company's positioning changes frequently from one vague or confusing story to another.

Making decisions that remove focus from the primary engine of your business is when things often go sideways. What feels like ambition becomes the organizational plaque that slows the company over time. You need clear delineation between core and non-core activities, between the core business and controlled experiments. And you need a strong execution engine around that core. If your company has yet to find its "one thing" and is struggling to compete in multiple markets, you may need to ask if there is something worth saving (see the section at the end of this chapter).

Here are two warning signs your company is lacking focus:

- **Warning sign #1: Winning fewer new customers.** When the needs of customers in new markets diverge from the needs of customers of your core market or business (i.e., different types of buyers need different packaging, features, pricing and services), going after them stretches your team and dilutes focus. Adding more bodies to build unproven products and go-to-market (GTM) strategies doesn't work. If you go from winning 40 percent of your deals to 25 percent, you're likely trying to expand too quickly into unfamiliar territory.

  - *Metrics to Watch:* increased CAC, lower win rate, lower conversion rates, lower sales rep productivity, slowed funnel velocity

- **Warning sign #2: Frustrated customers.** Great companies focus on one customer segment and work hard to win that segment—and thrill those customers—before moving on to other segments. If you move on too quickly from your core segment to other types of customers with different needs, you will likely suffer frustrated customers because you can't support all the requirements simultaneously. Those frustrated customers will then take up valuable time and may leave you anyway, while writing crappy reviews of you online.

  - *Metrics to Watch*: decreased customer satisfaction or net promoter score (NPS—how much your customers like the company), increased customer churn (percentage of customers that leave), decrease in customer lifetime value (LTV)

Much of this book is dedicated to understanding your core business and building a solid operational engine around that core. Focus is easy to grasp but hard to define when you're in the thick of it. I still make mistakes in this area. It requires constant attention.

Ask yourself the hard questions: Did a lack of focus lead to the issues you face today? Did you expand too quickly across too many fronts? Did you decisively win your initial "beachhead" market before moving on to the next market? How might things be different if you had expanded more slowly? Did you focus too many employees on unproven markets that failed to play out as expected?

Staying true to your core—your one thing—is tough to do, but when done well is the essence of long-term health. Only when you do will you have the time, space, and resources you need to discover your breakaway strategy.

PROBLEM 4: BUYING INTO A DISTORTED NARRATIVE

Being a good storyteller about what the business does, how it's doing, and where it's going is a foundational characteristic of great leaders. A strong narrative inspires employees, influences markets, and attracts customers. Startup leaders rely on storytelling to communicate data to stakeholders, connecting data points like a puzzle to justify decisions and defend positions (and often themselves).

But storytelling becomes wildly problematic when leaders believe their own fairy tales devoid of actual data to support them. Fueled by dreams of breakaway growth, overly optimistic stories that don't reflect reality become woven into decision-making. This problem is exacerbated when the story keeps changing alongside product and market shifts and when there isn't a concerted effort to align employees around the right story.

The ability to tell a good story can be more than just a weakness, as we saw in leaders like Elizabeth Holmes, the former CEO of Theranos, who was convicted of defrauding investors by claiming the company's non-functional technology was saving lives. The fine line between entrepreneurial optimism and outright lying gets blurred in the emotion-fueled push to succeed.

You may not be at a Theranos level of reality distortion but still suffer from the effects of buying into—and sharing—a distorted narrative. It is hard to recognize when it is happening. Still, the symptoms are apparent: (1) relying on a few data points as the basis for a trend, (2) misinterpreting the cause of events or outcomes, (3) maintaining an outdated story that no longer reflects reality, and (4) believing teammates who tell you what you want to hear.

Warning signs that you are peddling a distorted narrative include:

- **Warning sign #1: Stories vary across teams:** If salespeople look skeptical when you discuss your strength in a particular market, or if product managers wince at your vision because it's more ambitious than your roadmap, then you may be suffering from a narrative that is too far removed from the truth. Also, pay attention to how teams tell their own story (e.g., on customer calls or at all-hands meetings) and see how it aligns with your primary story.

  - *Metrics to Watch*: conflicting data points across teams and missed "primary" results (the major metrics that can't be obfuscated)

- **Warning sign #2: Missed operating plan:** The operating plan usually represents the best proof that your story is the right one and is playing out as expected. It will also be the primary source for the board to know if things are working.

- *Metrics to Watch*: the major 3–5 metrics for your business that drive your operating plan, such as new revenue, retention rate, conversion rate, delivery of new features on time, customer satisfaction, etc.

To assess how you got stuck, it's essential that you "power wash" old narratives to uncover the truth. Doing so keeps your team motivated and aligned, ensures your board stays connected to what matters, and supports success in your core market. It's time for a clean slate and a unifying story your whole company can get behind.

PROBLEM 5: FAILING TO MANAGE THROUGH DISRUPTIVE SHIFTS

Whether it's a new technology, a low-priced competitor, a novel business model from a new entrant, or a proliferation of niche vendors, even startups get pushed out of their market. Companies often get stuck trying to deal with the disruption.

The problem usually has less to do with disruption and more with the company's response to it. Founders attempt to "change the tires on a moving car" by changing their technology or business model while maintaining their core business. They can't figure out their place between the old and the new—and ultimately lose on both fronts. The more significant the disruption, the harder it is to pull off this multi-threaded approach, and the more critical it is to pick a lane and consider options like merging with a company that allows you to compete successfully in the new area.

These are the two warning signs that you are failing to manage through a disruptive shift productively:

- **Warning sign #1: Missed opportunities and customers.** It's usually apparent when a new entrant with better technology is winning over your market; but not always, especially if you have bought into a distorted narrative per #4 mentioned earlier. If you're a B2B company, you'll see more lost deals to the cheaper, better, and faster competitor. If you're B2C, you'll see it in purchase data, reviews, and feedback from channel partners.

  - *Metrics to Watch*: decreased win rate, increased churn, increased CAC, or return on ad spend (RoAS)

- **Warning sign #2: A new player taking the lower end of the market.** You may not be losing your core customers yet, but if new entrants are winning a part of the market that you don't focus on, it might be trouble down the line as they could catch up to you. For B2B businesses, this often takes the form of startups approaching small businesses first, then working their way up-market. For B2C, it's usually a company selling directly to customers and building up a strong brand, which is then pushed through other channels on a larger scale.

Assess What Happened—What Went Wrong? Is It Fixable?

> – ***Metrics to Watch***: decreased win rate on smaller
> deals, increased press and customer mentions of the
> new player, and changes in customer feedback scores

Technology and industry shifts force change. If you can't make the shift or leverage your core strengths to maintain your growth and win a new part of the market, it may be time to find a home for your business or distribute the remaining cash and wind down. Sometimes there isn't a great path for the company, and it's better to own that decision early rather than keep everyone on the same losing ride for the long run. I have made this mistake; it's a hard one to reconcile with, even years later.

TOM EISENMANN:
WHAT GOES WRONG IN STARTUPS

Tom Eisenmann is the go-to expert on why companies get stuck. He is the author of the must-read book *Why Startups Fail: A New Roadmap for Entrepreneurial Success* (New York: Currency, 2021), a practical and case study–rich overview of early and late-stage startup challenges. Tom is the Howard H. Stevenson Professor of Business Administration at the Harvard Business School, the Peter O. Crisp Chair of the Harvard Innovation Labs, and Faculty Co-Chair of the HBS Rock Center for Entrepreneurship, the Harvard MS/MBA Program, and the Harvard College Technology Fellows Program.

How do growth companies get off track?
One of the most significant risks is what I call the "Speed Trap" challenge, which affects later-stage startups that scale too

quickly. These companies raise funding based on success with an early adopter segment that is easy to acquire and loves the product. They then use that new capital to expand aggressively into market segments that are harder to penetrate and satisfy. By this time, they're burning cash, and competitors are entering the market with cheaper alternatives. Without options for more funding, growth grinds to a halt, and the company gets stuck.

What "people" issues do you see in growth companies?
A considerable challenge is gaps in the senior leadership team. Many startups fail to hire the right senior leaders and fall prey to competing priorities, cultural challenges, and heavy cash burn. When it takes three to six months to hire execs and three to six months to determine if they're doing the right job, the wrong hire could kill the company. There is also the cultural challenge of moving from a mission-driven, jack-of-all-trades team to hiring employees who see the work only as a job. Finally, the faster the company grows, the more likely it will be missing systems (e.g., planning, budgeting, and HR) to organize the employees, which slows progress and creates confusion.

What should startups with early traction do to improve their chances?
It's easy for an MBA professor to say, but more analysis is needed. Is there a risk of saturation in the core market? A company like Dropbox could scale to half a billion users with their main product before they scratch the surface of market saturation. But most companies need clever segmentation and careful cohort analysis to understand the market dynamics determining when and how to scale. They should also undertake an

executive audit to know how ready their team is for the next wave of growth and enlist as much support as possible in hiring the ideal executives for the next growth phase.

Is there a systemic, industry-wide problem with venture-backed startups?

For early-stage companies, we need more education to help founders do the homework before building. Many founders want to develop a product before validating the concept at a deep level, which leads to wasted effort and time. For later-stage startups, entrepreneurs must understand that raising VC means signing up to ride a rocket ship and that VCs generate their returns on a small percentage of the portfolio. A slow and steady approach with alternative investment sources might be a better path, but many founders don't understand those trade-offs until it's too late.

How do you counsel founders who are experiencing failure?

I first ask them about the runway: Are you out of moves? Are you miserable? Is there time to exit gracefully? Ideally, you have enough to provide severance, pay vendors, and run a responsible wind-down process. After it's done, you must process the pain and learn from what happened without ruminating on the failure or distracting yourself with the next new thing. Some of these "Speed Trap" companies can find a way to survive. It may be a failure for the original investors, but the company rises from the ashes and lives on under a different cap structure and growth expectations, and that can be rewarding for the founders.

What Kind of "Stuck" Are You?

Once you have a clear analysis of how you got stuck, you must consider your financial options for managing through a transformation. A stalled startup will fall into one of the following categories, each with different options for getting unstuck.

- **Stuck with no runway**: You have product and market challenges and need more funding. If you can't become profitable by shrinking your team or raising more money, you will be forced to close, sell, or recapitalize the business. The transformation will be best served by recapitalizing the company with new investors whose investment approach is aligned with your new plan. That will provide you with enough flexibility and a "clean slate" to rebuild using the process in this book.

- **Stuck with some runway**: The current business needs to be fixed, but you have enough cash for a year or two to figure things out. You need to manage that cash carefully. Pay close attention to the restructuring processes detailed in chapters 3 and 4, which might allow you to maintain a healthy company while running thoughtful growth experiments as described in chapter 5. It's a "go lean to fight another day" strategy that requires discipline and bold moves to use your cash most effectively.

- **Stuck and profitable**: You are making money (or have a clear path to becoming profitable) but don't have an obvious growth path. You can stay profitable and generate cash for investors—or you can run growth experiments to find a breakaway opportunity. Chapters 5 and 6 cover how to carefully test the waters to find the right path and how to make the hard decision of whether to pursue growth and at what rate.

It should be obvious which category your company falls into and the options available to salvage it. But before you can go through the hard work of getting your business unstuck, you need to figure out one final important piece: Is your company worth saving?

Can You Turn Things Around?

Now that you've assessed why you got stuck and what kind of "stuck" situation you're in, you can decide whether your company is worth saving. This requires deep reflection. Entrepreneurs often jump to action before deeply and honestly answering the hard questions. Our desire for movement gets us into trouble.

Over the years, I've collected a list of questions to determine whether you and your business can go through this transformation process successfully:

- **Are you excited about the future?** This is hands-down the most important question. You must have the conviction that you can transform this business. No one is ever 100 percent sure, but belief is paramount. If you can't say, "Hell yes, let's do this!" with confidence, you can skip the rest of the questions.

- **Is there a strong core?** What can your business do better than any company in the world that customers love? Brand, technology, team, channel relationships, knowledge of your category? Do customers love your offering? Having a fan base means there's hope—something special under the hood that can be used to create your second act. If you don't have any customers who need or love your product, it will be a hard ride.

- **How will you win?** Is there a market you can dominate? Can you get there from here? Has a new technology nullified your strategy? Once you know you have a strong core, the next challenge is applying that core to a genuine set of pain points on a larger scale. Beyond your core market, is there a chance to do more? If your market is crowded, how will you stand out? Will you need to create a new category or stay within your current category? Are customers asking (ideally begging) you for this new offering, or will it require education and pushing?

- **How much will it cost?** Can you afford to make this move? How much do you realistically need (with room for cushion) to architect the transformation? Can you do it with the existing cap structure? Are your investors behind you, or do you need to recapitalize the business with new investors? Be pragmatic when answering these questions and involve people who understand the financing options.

- **What is the end game?** Do you want to sell the

business? Take it public? Build a profitable annuity stream? No path is inherently wrong, and you don't necessarily want to focus only on outcomes. But problems arise when you aren't on the same page as your co-founders, leadership team, or investors about where the company should go. These conflicting exit goals can surface too late and cause unnecessary angst in the long run. Figure out the right path for the business together. If you can't get aligned, you'll need to recapitalize or restructure to ensure everyone's incentives are lined up for this stage.

It takes a metric ton of blood, sweat, and tears to get a startup unstuck. It requires a new strategy, team, culture, process, systems, philosophy, and approach. It may also require new capitalization and ownership. Deciding to rebuild should not be considered—and ultimately pursued—lightly.

Starting Over

If you decide it makes more sense to sell or wind down your business, let me put on my life coach hat for a moment. You'll get back on the horse. I've had plenty of failures (sometimes three or four at the same company), and somehow, like many other entrepreneurs, I keep getting up again. When we don't overly identify with the business's success or failure, we learn a lot each time and enjoy the ride more than the destination. Don't burn this book. Even if you're moving on to greener pastures, this book will help ensure your new venture is best positioned for breakout success.

Maybe you decide to start something new or acquire a business and make it more valuable. Or buy back a business you sold (or were forced out of) and breathe life into it again. A friend of mine started a company, sold it, bought it back, sold it again, then bought it back again, and now runs it profitably. You can spin out parts of your business, buy other spinouts, or merge companies together. The business world is a fluid river of opportunity. Things may suck now, but fortunes change quickly. Vision, heart, and discipline are the tools to ensure you stay on the river and don't get stuck in an eddy of regret and stasis.

Whatever the outcome, if your business fails, you are not a failure. I still struggle with this concept, but I know it in my heart to be true. You are not your business. You connect with a purpose, assemble a team, and bring a new idea to the world, and you leave it all on the field, trying to make it work. Maybe you do that just once, maybe many times. But separate the results from your self-worth. As Muhammad Ali said, "Inside of a ring or out, ain't nothing wrong with going down. It's staying down that's wrong."

Your mental state is the most important factor in the path of our companies. You need to be at the top of your game to assemble the team, build a vision, and make the right decisions. That's why the first step is to own your missteps and ensure you are coming at this with the right mindset, which we'll cover in the next chapter.

Hard Lessons

In 2017, itching for a new project and lacking the patience to wait for the right one, I acquired a company called Ice.com. Ice was an online jewelry retailer that was founded in 1999 by two brothers back when e-commerce was taking off. Their family had been in the jewelry-manufacturing business for more than 30 years, so they saw the rise of e-commerce as an opportunity to eliminate the middlemen and sell high-end jewelry at a lower cost directly to consumers. Soon, Ice.com was a favorite of the dot.com boom. The brothers went on to raise $50 million in funding and grow the company aggressively for nine years—until the economy tanked in 2008.

Overnight, the company went from $80 million in sales to $10 million. After that, it changed hands multiple times and turned into a low-price seller of commodity jewelry. The magic that made the company special was lost through years of profit-squeezing. It was an empty shell of a company competing on price. There was nothing special about this business—nothing that customers loved to drive loyalty. When I bought the company, I envisioned transforming it through the smarter use of data. But no amount of data-driven growth hacking can dig you out of a business with no core.

Getting to profitability meant making serious cuts, which we eventually did, and building our own private-label products. While the company was no longer bleeding cash, it was stuck—earning a small amount but not enough to reinvest. We had figured out a way to use new technology to build a disruptive "demand-sensing" engine for real-time jewelry sales, but it would have required a healthy injection of new capital and a lot of my time to build a big business out of the ashes of this old one. Also, I had no passion for the jewelry industry, which should have been a red flag.

The business had to be sold. Any transformation would essentially entail starting from scratch. After a year of trying for smart growth, we sold the business in a less-than-ideal transaction (however, we did sell the domain for the largest domain sale in 2018, which lessened the pain).

I was reminded that not all companies can be saved. You need to consider carefully whether you can realistically take on the great challenge of turning around a company. And if not, on to the next one!

Become the Leader Your Company Needs Now– Transform Yourself to Transform the Company

We cannot change anything unless we accept it.

—CARL JUNG

Jesse Pujji was miserable.

The Founding CEO of Ampush, a social media marketing company, Jesse and his team had bootstrapped their startup into a large company. But now it was struggling. And *he* was struggling. He hated going to work. The culture had deteriorated, and he was personally getting bad reviews on Glassdoor. Like the company, he was stuck.

Jesse was born and raised in St. Louis, the son of a hardcharging father with high expectations. Since he was young,

Jesse put pressure on himself to be successful. That drive got him through the University of Pennsylvania's Wharton Business School undergrad program, then to McKinsey, then to Goldman Sachs. And he eventually founded Ampush with two close friends in 2010.

Ampush (an amalgam of the first two letters of each founder's last name) served as a customer acquisition provider for companies like Uber, Dollar Shave Club, Peloton, and Blue Apron. Jesse directed all his intense, achievement-oriented energy into his company, pushing hard for growth. In the early days, this worked, creating a rapidly growing and successful company. But that energy was now driving a wedge between him and his employees.

After five years of hard work, Jesse was burnt out. He tried to sell the company but failed, adding to his "sad and tired" state of mind. Instead, he sold a portion of his equity to Red Ventures, a unique holding company, putting millions in his pocket. It was a wonderful life moment. But now that he had achieved some financial success, the underlying problem worsened as his motivation faltered. A fear of failure had fueled his early egoic drive. With money in the bank and a great family at home, he began to feel rudderless. He had lost his commitment and purpose. He wanted to be done with the company.

He called Ric Elias, the founder and CEO of Red Ventures, and shared his truth. Ric responded in his caring but firm tone, "Jesse, you are one of the luckiest dudes I know! Barely 30, two beautiful kids, personally wealthy, and you call all the shots," he told him. "Stop acting like the company owns you; you own the company. Make it a vessel for your personal growth and the growth of your people."

Ric encouraged Jesse to get a coach. Initially reluctant, Jesse agreed. He began working with Dave Kashen, a long-time CEO coach, and threw himself into the inner work, which soon produced two profound insights:

1. He approached his work from a "should" mentality, not a "want" mentality. He was a dutiful but reluctant leader and brought a heavy martyr energy to his work. He was motivated by a fear of not being successful, which was slowly eating away his power.

2. He was disconnected from his purpose. He no longer felt the meaning behind his work, which hindered his motivation. Selling ads wasn't exactly curing cancer. Is this how he wanted to spend his life?

Armed with these insights, Jesse reengineered his perspective on why and how he showed up as a leader. He was determined to get back his mojo.

First, he realized that what got him up in the morning was growing people. "I was so focused on getting the answer right that I forgot why I was doing it in the first place," he told me. "Fear was leading my actions instead of my passion: developing people. What if I used business challenges to help my team grow instead of criticizing them for not getting it right?"

Second, he discovered that context was more important than content when it came to purpose. Using his company as the vessel to deliver his gift of growing people is a profound purpose, regardless of what the company sells. A healthy business that develops its employees into great people is precious to society and a deep fuel source for its leaders.

Jesse was bringing renewed focus, optimism, and health to his leadership. His team noticed. "When things go wrong now, you still address it and even use the same language," an employee told him. "But now, when you say it, I feel inspired rather than belittled. Like everything is going to be okay."

The business started to change, at first culturally and then financially. As it stabilized and the growth path became clear, Jesse had another profound insight: the company needed a different leader. Thanks to his inner work, he knew he was not the operationally minded leader—the "carry a clipboard and keep the trains running on time" CEO—the business needed at that point in its journey. In 2020, Jesse moved into the chairman role as a new CEO came on board. It was a perfect fit, and three years later, the company was acquired in an excellent outcome for everyone.

Upon stepping down as CEO, Jesse founded Gateway X, a venture studio to focus on the "creation" side of startups, coaching founders and working across multiple projects. The work was born from his greatest strengths of creating new ideas and coaching others. And he's never been happier.

Getting (Yourself) Unstuck

Whenever I meet second- or third-time founders like Jesse, I ask them: "What do you wish you had known early on?" Most say they wished they could have gotten out of their own way sooner. Many had to kill a company before they understood their blind spots and motivations and how to change their approach. The lesson that kept coming up in my conversations with experienced entrepreneurs was:

Your business won't transform until you do.

You may be tempted to write this concept off as Pollyanna psychobabble. I assure you it's not. Like people who repeatedly get into bad relationships because they won't confront their issues, you will run into the same scaling problems unless you understand and work through your and your team's systemic deficiencies. Knowing your blind spots often means the difference between failure and triumph.

If the previous chapter asks, "Can this business be saved?" this chapter asks, "What is the right mindset to save it?" Rearchitecting your company for greatness will require your best selves.

To do that, you must be willing to (1) do a thorough analysis of your strengths, weaknesses, and motivations and (2) commit to transforming yourself as a leader.

What Makes You Great?

How would you convince people to follow you into battle if you only had 30 seconds? What are your and your leadership team's unique core strengths that will sustain you through the dark forest of startup transition and growth?

When you take on a business transformation, you're on the precipice of a years-long project that can be thankless, painful, and slow. You need conviction. Confidence will waiver, but you must believe in your company's destiny.

This starts with understanding your strengths. What got you and your company to its early success? What fueled you and your team to push forward when hit with the painful slings and arrows of market reality? To get you started, here are the traits most leadership studies suggest successful entrepreneurs share—

- Honest
- Strategic
- Results-driven
- Confident
- Resilient
- Focused
- Purposeful/inspiring
- Decisive/solution-driven
- Visionary/innovative
- Empathic
- Customer-focused
- Humble

Read your old performance reviews and feedback from employees and teammates, and write down your top three to five strengths. Your goal is to identify the unique character-istics that best represent you and that would place you in the top 10 percent of all leaders. For example, you might write something like this to describe why you think "strategic" is a strength:

Strategic: *Thanks to my years as a strategy consultant, my col-leagues rated me as an outstanding strategic facilitator. Some of the most critical business decisions in my last three companies were made with me behind the whiteboard marker.*

Why is understanding your unique strengths important? Because:

- The company needs people operating in their "power alley" to have the best shot at building a breakaway company.

- You'll be happier and more motivated when operating from your strengths. The energy that comes from being good at your job allows you to work long days and get the fuel of positive feedback.

- Understanding when you're at your best helps you to identify and surround yourself with the right team of complementary professionals.

An awareness of our strengths can also illuminate our blind spots, since our greatest strengths typically have a shadow side. For instance, an empathetic leader garners loyalty but can also be a "helicopter parent" who tries to save the day instead of inspiring people to deal with it on their own.

What Are Your Strengths' Shadow Sides?

In 2007, Edwin A. Locke, a psychologist at the forefront of goal theory, and J. Robert Baum, a business professor focused on entrepreneurship, studied the traits, values, and motives of successful startup leaders. Among many common strengths they found in entrepreneurs—independence, self-confidence, drive, tenacity, etc.—was "egoistic passion" or a focus on proving themselves through their work.[4]

As Locke and Baum explain, entrepreneurs typically don't have big egos but rather fragile, inflated ones. They often suffer from self-doubt, which leads them to spend much time trying to prove themselves—to relieve that doubt. People with high self-esteem don't need constant approval or compare themselves to others. They don't need to earn love through their achievements.

Entrepreneurs have many traits to be grateful for: We can deal with stress and chaos while remaining unwavering in our determination to succeed. We can get rejected by 50 investors before finding the right one. But our insecurities can get the best of us and drive us toward behaviors like not asking for help, micromanaging, or raising more money than we need. This is true whether you are a non-CEO founder, a founding CEO, or a hired CEO.

If you had asked what drove me as an entrepreneur in my

---

4   Robert J. Baum, Michael Frese, and Robert A. Baron, eds. *The Psychology of Entrepreneurship* (New York: Psychology Press, 2013).

twenties, I probably would have stumbled through an answer like, "I want to leave my mark and lead a creative team of people on a mission." I wouldn't have said, "I must earn the love I want through my achievements and financial success." But that would have been closer to the truth.

If we haven't confronted the shadow sides of our strengths—those destructive mindsets that tend to trip us leaders and entrepreneurs up—they will *always* find a way to haunt us.

FOUR DESTRUCTIVE MINDSETS

Over the years of working at and with startups, I have identified four mindsets that are particularly dangerous in startup leaders:

- **Insecurity:** Insecurity can be a common problem among younger founders. Their drive to build a company is strong but comes from needing to prove themselves to friends, family, and business connections. This leads to decisions that "look good" but aren't in the long-term best interests of the company, such as raising too much money, putting too much money into PR (so they show off their coverage in popular content channels), or focusing on vanity metrics that don't have a deep impact on the success of the business. Insecurity can derail companies quickly, especially when it promotes scaling prematurely.

  - *Warning Signs*: You focus on how actions will be perceived rather than the outcomes; your narratives on how the company is doing are overly glowing; you talk more than you listen.

- **Greed:** Greed is a desire to acquire more than one needs. It affects leaders who have seen success and want to use their position to "dominate a market." They have lost sight of their purpose (why their company exists), unique strengths, and thoughtful growth. They instead see the market only as the means to win. This blind allegiance to winning can translate into targeting customers who aren't a good fit, hiring too many people, charging customers more than is fair, or in extreme cases, even breaking laws. Greed is a destructive pursuit that burns out the team, corrupts the culture, wastes money, and confuses the strategy and execution.

  - *Warning Signs*: Your strategic plans are optimized around dollar amounts instead of long-term growth; you create cultural challenges by fostering a dog-eat-dog environment that rewards selfish interests over company priorities.

- **Hubris:** Hubris is corrupt selfishness, overconfidence, and pride. It's the opposite of humility. It drives leaders to overestimate their abilities and put their desires before the welfare of others. Hubris urges leaders to enact highly improbable strategies despite data that suggests they will fail. Hubris can be well disguised but often leads to recklessness and a "reality distortion field" that drives poor decisions and a toxic culture.

- *Warning Signs*: Your team is sycophantic and overly agreeable; employees complain about hostile working conditions; you make too many decisions on your own; your grand plans rarely come to fruition.

• **Envy:** Envy is a deep desire for the traits or possessions of others. When leaders see peers in the press or hear stories of their breakout success, they want to measure up. Instead of engaging in thorough competitive analysis and calculated market strategy, they focus on copying or beating out rivals or keeping up with peers. This leads to emotional decisions that can kill innovation and positioning. Instead of having a unique point of view, they become a copycat on the road to average . . . or a dead cat on the side of the road.

- *Warning Signs*: Your strategy is overly optimized around one competitor; market share is your primary metric; you seek milestones based on appearances rather than what the business needs (e.g., closing a large but unnecessary funding round).

These mindsets tend to be more prevalent in younger founders, but they can arise anytime in our professional lives. Ensuring they are not affecting our decisions requires constant monitoring. This is no small task. These mindsets often play out in small ways that are hard to notice. For example, out of hubris, a leader might underestimate the time required to launch a new product despite having data to the contrary—what is known as the "planning fallacy," which leads to the business getting stuck.

These mindsets are often the motivations behind some of the labels and names our employees use to describe us, such as—

- **Over-optimist:** Ignores lousy news, hoping it will go away.

- **Control freak:** Micromanages the team into frustration and stasis.

- **Drill sergeant:** Creates a culture of "what have you done for me lately."

- **Smartest in the room:** Needs to have all the answers and downplays others' ideas.

- **Savior:** Wants to rescue people in trouble, and sometimes the entire company, for the sake of their identity.

- **Checklist-lover:** Sees work as a set of tasks; can't see the bigger picture.

- **Egoist:** Sees the business as an extension of their identity and doesn't trust others to make decisions.

- **Moderator:** Wants people to like them, so includes everyone in every decision and has trouble making decisions.

- **Gambler:** Shoots first and asks questions later.

- **Hummingbird:** Flits from one project to another without seeing them through.

- **Miser:** Afraid to spend money, so starves the business of needed resources.

- **Salesperson:** Promotes an exaggerated version of the truth to employees, customers, and investors.

- **Specialist:** Understands one part of the business well and spends all their time there.

- **Analyst:** Analyzes every decision and forces their team to justify everything.

- **Sloth:** Goes on autopilot after some success, lowering expectations for themselves, their people, and the company.

I have been some version of these archetypes at various times. It can be hard to own our negative behaviors, but it is profoundly cathartic when we do, especially when we open up with our colleagues.

Following your strengths, list your top three to five blind spots. Using the earlier archetypes or old performance reviews to guide you, paint a picture of the traits or behaviors that have driven you to make poor decisions in the past and have the highest potential to derail your success moving forward. For example, here is what you might write about the shadow side of your "strategic" strength—

Moderator: My years of consulting turned me into a facilitator of group decisions instead of an intuitive leader who makes hard decisions to keep the company moving quickly. This has led to long, drawn-out decision-making processes, confused employees, and poor company execution.

As you complete your list, think about leaders you have worked for in the past. How did they rub you the wrong way?

Do you share those shortcomings? Did you inherit cultural norms from previous companies?

The complete list of your strengths and weaknesses will constitute your Leadership Profile, a frank assessment of the inner challenges that affect your decision-making and management style. It's remarkable how little we know about our weaknesses when we're in the flow of work. Even if we get feedback, we have difficulty accepting it or changing our approach. That's why enlisting the help of people who know you well is paramount. If you have a spouse or partner, for example, getting their input is gold, as they are likely the best at seeing through your baggage.

Alternatively, have a third party conduct a 360-degree review with past and current team members. Reading the results of that review is enlightening. CEOs I've coached who have done 360-degree assessments still refer to those documents years later, recognizing them as powerful turning points in their lives and reading them repeatedly to prevent themselves from slipping into old patterns.

KIRBY WINFIELD:
GETTING DERAILED BY PRIDE

Kirby Winfield, Founding General Partner at Ascend.vc, a pre-seed stage venture fund in Seattle, is also a deeply experienced operator, having been on the founding teams of two public start-ups—Go2Net and Marchex—and CEO of two venture-backed companies, AdXpose (acquired by comScore) and Dwellable (acquired by HomeAway). But beyond having a great resume, he's a great human being with hard-won insights about the founder's journey. He has seen the path from every angle and now uses that wisdom to help others navigate it.

What drove you in the early days of your career?

I came into the work world with the mantra, "Show up first, leave last, and ask for more." My first company, Go2Net, had a 14-hour-day, Wall Street energy, which played right into my childhood need to achieve. I would run through walls and make others run through them with me. If I were going to fail, it wouldn't be for lack of hard work. I wanted to cut off that avenue of failure. It wasn't sustainable, but I wouldn't have been successful without that drive. The issue was that my entire identity was my work. I felt I needed to succeed on a large scale to earn the respect of my family, friends, and even my wife. I believed people loved me for my achievements, not who I was.

How did that drive affect your decision-making?

My first CEO role was at AdXpose. I led the business using that same work ethic. We raised a lot of venture money and brute-forced a revenue stream. But it was crappy, unsustainable ad network revenue. Over time, it became clear that we could transform the business and build a recurring SaaS model. But because *I* had built that early revenue stream, I was too proud to let it go. In a way, it was "my revenue." We had an early lead and could have captured the value of the market, but I couldn't get out of my way. The business never broke out. It was a classic sunk-cost fallacy. The next closest competitor, which was tiny when we were growing, pursued a more scalable, repeatable SaaS model and was eventually sold for $400 million. We were the only business out of four in that market that didn't succeed on a large scale. And it was due to my pride.

continued

How do you reflect on it now?

I was so "on tilt" then that I couldn't think clearly. My transformation was a result of these experiences. I saw that a good leader is a more balanced, humble individual. I recently wrote down my values to share with my son: Be honest with yourself, be kind to yourself, have a positive mental attitude, seek new opportunities, train daily, set goals to achieve them, show love, and share your feelings. As a young leader, I wasn't doing any of those things, so I couldn't effectively guide my companies. I had to learn from experience, and failure was a part of that. But now, having had that journey is my edge. Those mistakes made me a better investor, advisor, and coach.

How do you now coach founders to develop?

My advice is to slow down. Entrepreneurs are sprinting to find their thing and trying to grow when they shouldn't. Take a breath, pick something, do it, and see what happens. If people like it, do more of it. If you have a customer, work with them, get a few other customers, and see where it goes. Doing so is strategic because you can back-load your growth leading up to the next fundraise, but more importantly, it keeps you healthy for the marathon that is the startup journey. Not everyone is ready for the journey, so I look for healthy founders who can go the distance and adopt those values I learned the hard way.

What Role Did You Play in Your Company Getting Stuck?

Once you've identified your Leadership Profile—your strengths and weaknesses—analyze how you contributed to your company's stalled state. What led you to strategic decisions? Why did you raise (or not raise) the funding you did? Why did you hire the wrong people? Why can't (or couldn't) you get along with your partners? Are you still motivated to run this company? Understanding the destructive mindsets behind your actions is challenging and often requires the assistance of peers, friends, advisors, coaches, and possibly even therapists. It will be uncomfortable, often emotional work. But it is paramount to transforming your business. Confronting these issues is a process that should always continue. Dee Hock, the founder of Visa, said that great leaders should invest 40 percent of their time managing themselves: their "ethics, character, principles, purpose, motivation and conduct."[5]

These motivations are all too frequently *behind* the primary reason your company isn't breaking out. When we dissect our company's failure, we usually focus on external, strategic, or operational reasons like "not enough market demand," "we got blindsided by a new technology," or "we had the wrong team." We rarely examine our leadership and conclude that the company failed because "I wanted to control every decision, and this pushed out our best people who could have rebuilt our product using modern technology." It's our job to figure out what's behind the curtain of failure.

For example, as mentioned in the Introduction, my most recent leadership inner work was around being a savior. I identified as a hero who rescued others and did whatever it took to

---

5   M. Mitchell Waldrop, "Dee Hock on Management: Dee Hock's Management Principles, in His Own Words," Fast Company, October 31, 1996, https://www. fastcompany.com/27454/dee-hock-management.

make things work. (It's no accident that I'm in the turnaround business.) However, this destructive mindset led to doing more of the work than I should (rescuing people) and prolonging the lifespans of companies beyond their ideal path. I had to rewire this impulse through therapy, books, coaching, workshops, and, most importantly, by being honest with my team about these shortcomings and the reality of the businesses. Now, I know that *everyone* is better served if you can move on sooner instead of continuing to fix something that will be forever broken.

Engaging in your inner work—a (hopefully) powerful analysis of your strengths, weaknesses, and motivations—will serve several purposes:

- Ensure you are the right person to run the company now.

- Highlight your important development areas.

- Avoid the traps that got the company stuck.

- Enlist the right executives to balance your blind spots.

- Provide your coach (if you have one) with a guide for your development areas.

This analysis is like excavating your root structure to become the right leader—what Jim Collins, author of *Good to Great*, calls a Level 5 Leader: someone whose ambition is for the institution, not him or herself. Doing the hard inner work on yourself is the most important thing you can do for a successful business transformation.

Becoming a Transformation Leader

Keeping employees happy and busy, finding new customers, recruiting people for your cause, and keeping your energy up takes unique qualities. Over the years, I've found the following attributes ideal to drive a successful transformation:

- **Purpose-driven:** The whirlwind of success can sometimes detract from the "why" behind your efforts. Getting unstuck is a lot easier when you have an unwavering belief in how you're making the world better. A commitment to purpose is your most efficient fuel source as a leader.

- **Others-focused:** In a turnaround, your needs take a back seat to those of your employees and customers. Without the luxury of the market "pulling" you into hypergrowth, your role is to reground the company around its new mission and put yourself on the front lines. This requires servant leadership.

- **Resilient:** During boom times, you are drowning in positive feedback and buoyed by success. When you're stuck, that goes away. People stop taking your calls. You don't get asked to give inspiring talks at events. Employees you've laid off trash the company online. You're subject to bad news (and possibly lousy press). It may be a while before you feel on top again. You need thick skin.

- **Precise:** When the business is going well, decisions, data, and clarity can get muddled amid the fog of growth.

Details and negative data may get swept under the rug of success. Now you must watch every decision. You must be vigilant, objective, and focused to get through this stage.

- **Thrifty:** You might not have scrutinized the purse strings after funding rounds, but now there's no option. Cut the fancy offsites, kombucha kegs, and launch parties, and no more kowtowing to execs who whine for more hires. You must spend time on the budget and get creative with resources—give out more equity than cash compensation; give up your office space; and consider contract-to-hire agreements.

- **Humble:** You're not a market-leading powerhouse (yet). This is a time to listen and be open to ideas about the company's future. Your primary responsibility is the transformation process, not necessarily the content of how you will succeed—the best ideas will likely not come from you. So check your ego and become a "receiver" of ideas and information. You are a steward of transformation. You are not the company.

Which of these qualities do you have? Which of these will you need to breathe new life into your company? Make a list and hold it dear, because these qualities will be the guardrail against the decisions that have gotten you stuck in the past. With that in place, you can develop yourself as a leader.

Developing Your Leadership Skills

Now that you have an overview of who you are and who you need to be as a leader to guide your team during this next phase of work, it's time to develop a leadership style that will serve during the rebuilding process. The goal is not to transform yourself into a new person overnight, but to have a more profound sense of your authentic leadership style. There are several ways to develop your leadership skills:

- **Work with a coach:** A coach will help you design a growth path, navigate big decisions, and sound the alarm when you fall back into old patterns. If hiring a coach is not feasible, build a roadmap of the qualities and skills you want to develop and find a mentor to help.

- **Read:** Ask peers and advisors for book recommendations on areas where you want to grow. Want to become a more empathetic leader? Become better at building teams? Become a servant leader? There are great books and quality resources online (podcasts, classes, apps, etc.) on leadership topics. You can also start a mini book club and read books with your team. I've found that to be a bonding activity, a motivator, and a source of ideas and decisions.

- **Complement your skills:** Consider your team's composition. Are your team members a good balance of your strengths and abilities? Or are you surrounded by people with similar characteristics? It's vital to the transformation path to have a well-rounded team.

- **Ask your team for help**: Enlisting your team in your leadership transformation is a great way to showcase vulnerability and speed up your growth. Have them call you out if they see old behaviors and reward them for doing so. Your efforts will create deeper relationships while inspiring the team to develop themselves.

Whether you are a founder or a new leader at your company, preparing for transformation involves the same process of self-assessment, acceptance, and commitment to becoming the best leader your company needs *now*.

Personal Board of Directors

A friend of mine, Raj Kapoor, is a successful entrepreneur. He was a co-founder of Snapfish, a venture capitalist with Mayfield, the chief strategy officer of Lyft, and now is a general partner for Climactic, a VC fund focused on climate startups.

In 2013, Raj founded FitMob, a marketplace for live fitness classes. A few years later, he pivoted to a subscription network that allowed users to sign up for classes at participating studios. FitMob went head-to-head against ClassPass, a more extensive network of studios. ClassPass had gotten to market much earlier and was gaining traction, spreading like fire across the country. FitMob had pivoted into this market too late and didn't have the resources to keep up with the viral growth of ClassPass.

Still, Raj fought tooth and nail to win market share and believed he would emerge as the winner. After all, he was a seasoned entrepreneur and VC while a younger first-timer ran ClassPass. He was convinced his experience would lead him to eventual victory. Raj was a fantastic salesperson, which served him well in his career. However, his ability to persuade people got him in trouble when he convinced *himself* and others that FitMob would win—while ignoring the clear signs that it had already lost.

Luckily, Raj could rely on a group of advisors—peers and professional friends who knew him well and knew his strengths and blind spots. They took him aside and said, "You need to let go of your ego. You're selling yourself a false narrative. There's a time to fight and a time to surrender."

In 2015, FitMob merged with ClassPass, and Raj worked for their CEO for six months to help integrate the companies and continue their expansion. "I had to put my ego down and go to my competitor, a company we had viciously fought with for years, and give them the keys. It took everything I had, but it was the right call," he told me. "If I didn't have my friends and spiritual advisors to help, I would have kept blindly fighting."

Like Raj, I recommend you assemble a group of advisors to help you get out of your own way. This "personal board of directors" knows you well and enables you to make hard decisions. Unlike a company's board of directors, a personal board is accountable to *you*, not investors or shareholders. It holds you to your values and purpose and helps you make smarter decisions. And yet, your board is not focused on specific company issues as they don't have all the data or context. They are not company advisors—they are *your* advisors. You don't want them to get emotionally invested in your company's success. It's okay to receive business feedback, but you must focus your board on personal development.

Want to rebalance your life? Talk to the board. Write a book? Board. Become a goat herder in Bhutan? Therapist first, then your board.

Close friends and family will love you no matter what, but they're generally overly supportive. You need tough love from people who know you well professionally, have had similar journeys, hold you to high standards, and help you connect the dots between your values and complicated professional decisions. And hopefully, they inspire you.

Loneliness and solitary thinking can be brutal, even after your company becomes an 800-pound gorilla. Having people there for you who know you is the best way to ensure you're growing, learning, and making good decisions.

Reconnect with Your Company's Soul

We typically begin our leadership journey with external motivations (e.g., how others perceive us). But as we grow, we learn the importance of an internal lens and mature into a more authentic leadership style as we rely less on external factors for our fulfillment. Doing so requires turning inward, analyzing our patterns, understanding how they got us into trouble, and recalibrating for the journey ahead.

Ideally, the human journey moves toward the soul and away from the ego (i.e., the roles we were told would provide the love we needed) as our internal compass. As children, we learn to use our ego to escape hard situations and provide a sense of belonging. As we age, however, those tactics begin to hold us back from living fully, and we must find a more bottomless well of energy to draw from in serving our purpose. If we don't transform, we risk our health and happiness and seek refuge in addiction, aggression, distraction, and isolation.

Businesses are the same. If a company's soul cannot flourish, it will slowly die. Employees will feel unease and lose connection with the mission as they no longer feel safe and in alignment with the organization. Customers, too, will sense the company's motivations and seek alternatives. The company's life energy will slowly dissipate.

A company's soul is in direct connection to the authenticity of its leader(s). A stuck company was likely held back by limiting mindsets, which must be confronted and acknowledged to move to the next phase. The secret is to combine youthful energy with learned wisdom. Only then can we build the company of our dreams.

Your company can't transform until you do.

Hard Lessons

Many years ago, I started a company called RipFog with some friends. The name was a portmanteau of Fog City (San

Francisco, where I was) and Rip City (Portland, where they were), though 95 percent of the people could only call it RipFrog, which seemed to be a better name. The idea behind the company was to bring cutting-edge technology to mobile backend infrastructure for companies with hugely popular, data-intensive mobile applications.

We raised $1 million in seed funding and hired a team to build the product. However, after six months of building, selling, and iterating, it became clear that customers weren't ready for what we were selling. What they had was good enough, and newer tech wasn't enough to get them to switch. We were just getting started but already stuck.

The problem was that I had hired people who were great at building but not as experienced at figuring out what to build. Compounding this situation was that this was before reliable videoconferencing, so we couldn't meet easily unless I flew up there every week, which was hard on the family and expensive for the company, and I was the primary idea guy.

I could have returned the money to the investors and said, "We got some false positives, but the market wasn't as big or ready as we had hoped." But mentally, I was deathly afraid of failure. I believed the company *was* me; if it failed, I was a failure. I scrambled for a viable business model to save the day—a wild-eyed lunatic hunting for product/market fit.

It eventually reached the breaking point of cash burn, with no business to back it up. And I was becoming wildly destructive to myself for failing. I had crippling back pain. But I found a buyer who needed the strong team we had assembled and "acqui-hired" the company for stock. The day after, I told the team the situation, which, while not ideal, they understood. The back pain was gone. The path was over.

In a positive twist, the team who went over to the new company had a great experience, and investors made a small return on the capital they invested after it was sold a few years later.

It took me a long time to figure out how to separate myself from the business while maintaining the motivation to build something meaningful. If I overly identified with the business and its outcomes, I got into egoic traps meant to protect my self-image, which hurt the company. Over time, I let the company's energy flow through me instead of being me. I was just a steward.

CHAPTER 3

Get Focused— Reorganize around Your Core

> You wanna fly, you got to give up the
> shit that weighs you down.
>
> —TONI MORRISON, *Song of Solomon*

Chase Franklin was at a crossroads.

Should he and his team wind down the business they had built over the previous three years and distribute whatever cash was left after paying off all the debts? Or should they try to sell the business—a task that seemed almost impossible in 2000, given the glut of companies for sale following the burst of the dot.com bubble?

Chase founded QPass in 1997 to help media companies

sell inexpensive digital content online through "micro-transactions." The company had patented a method that aggregated large blocks of small transactions and processed them in bulk so media companies could save on fees—and QPass would keep a percentage of the savings. If the *New York Times* wanted to sell crossword puzzles online, standard credit card processing fees would have been too expensive.

After a few years of business and a significant amount of venture funding, the company was doing $6 million in revenue, with $3.5 million coming from a single client, the *Wall Street Journal*. But this was the height of the first internet boom, so despite the small, shaky revenue, QPass was encouraged to raise another $90 million and was fast-tracked to go public. However, as they were gearing up to go public in 2000, the market crashed, and investors started asking hard questions.

They had promised billions of daily transactions but, at this point, were only processing about 6,000 a month. The reality was that most customers were experimenting with this new technology, not using it at scale. So when the economy collapsed and companies tightened expenses, QPass was among the first to be cut. Chase's vision of billions of tiny digital transactions hadn't come to fruition, and investors wanted a way out.

The company kept the core product team but was "running on fumes" with the remaining cash while Chase carefully weighed the options: wind down or sell? In early 2001, he considered a third option: reinvent the business. He wanted another chance.

But what could QPass do that the world needed? Chase knew its core was understanding and facilitating small digital transactions. But who needed that now?

Enter an unexpected opportunity: During the economic downturn, mobile carriers and data plans were exploding—it was the birth of broadscale mobile as devices became less expensive and networks became more reliable. And these large wireless companies were suddenly feeling the acute pain of processing small transactions. Why? It's hard to imagine now, but buying ringtones was huge. People wanted Justin Timberlake to alert them that their BFF was calling. And those small purchases needed infrastructure: a catalog of millions of products and customer service tools to manage who bought what and when.

Chase believed QPass could rebuild its product as a software platform for managing this new world of micro-commerce. He and the team took to the whiteboard. They created a re-imagined business of selling middleware (software that sits between operating systems and applications) embedded deep into the back-office of mobile carriers.

First, he had to convince the board to recap the business, and then he needed an investor with lots of risk tolerance. After 70 meetings, he finally found one. QPass cobbled together $12 million on a $3.5 million pre-money valuation—a shadow of its former valuation—but it needed a recapitalization and enough runway to get a new product to market. The new strategy was on.

QPass went from 220 employees to 50 and released the remaining old customers. The new culture became strong with the leaner team and new mission. "It was no longer about building a unicorn," Chase told me, "but about surviving as a successful business."

They were lean, driven, and focused. They spent only on what was needed to bring their new product to market, which they finally did in 2003. Their first customer was Cingular. Followed by AT&T. And then just about every major carrier. Over the next several years, QPass grew its revenue from $5 million to $40 million. They were on plan for $76 million when they were acquired for $330 million in 2006, just three years after the reboot.

"Our big insight," explains Chase, "was that our core business was not technology— which had to be rebuilt—or market position—since we had no more customers—but knowledge. We knew how to build a large-scale marketplace for digital goods and services; no one else did. The market opened for us in a time when most businesses went away."

What Is Your Core?

Understanding your core business is more challenging than it sounds, as most startups need to do a lot of experimentation in the early days to find the elusive "product/market fit." But as that fit becomes clear and the core solidifies, the experimentation-based approach leads to confusion if it is not tightly managed.

In traditional business parlance, "core business" is defined as the main activities that drive profit (e.g., manufacturing process, how it acquires customers). I don't find this very helpful for startups; so instead, I define it as the primary business the company is in and, ideally, what it is the best at. "Core business," in other words, is *the essence of a company's health and competitive advantage, which may be based on product, market position, relationships, business model, brand, capability, or critical insights into customers.* It is almost always the force behind the economic engine of the business.

Apple's core business is designing and marketing beloved consumer technology, Google's is search advertising, and Hershey's is consumer-packaged chocolate. These companies engage in other non-core activities—like Google's foray into self-driving cars or Hershey acquiring healthy snack companies—that might support future growth. But these companies can afford to do so because they have the infrastructure. The success of their core business gives them the brand, infrastructure, relationships, and insights to venture into other categories.

Often, market forces compel companies to move away from their historical core and orchestrate a transformation to survive in a new reality. Nokia, for example, started as a paper mill in the 1800s before going on to rubber boots, electricity, cable, and telecom equipment, then mobile phones in the late eighties, and now back to telecom equipment. You could make the case that Nokia's actual "core business" was not the products but the process of assembling products around a market need that got them through those business transformations.

Why is the concept of a "core business" so important? Because as startups find their core business—what they can be the best in the world at—they often begin to scale prematurely. They often continue experimenting with product/market fit while simultaneously trying to scale. Hungry for growth, they seek out shiny new opportunities beyond their core and before their core is solidified, not sensing that the distraction of constantly changing GTM strategies will cause pain later.

Many experienced founders and leaders I've talked to point to this distraction as the main reason startups get stuck. These companies figured out their core but didn't build up enough people, processes, and systems around that core to capitalize on the market opportunity. They never build a strong foundation for the business. They fight on too many fronts and can't organize effectively. Not having the patience to focus on bringing the core to fruition is a common regret of their leaders.

Transforming a stuck company requires clear reorganization around its core. Why? A defensible position in a smaller target market puts you in a solid financial place while positioning you for a breakaway move. First, however, you must understand and articulate your business core.

Finding Your Core

In stuck companies, the core is often blurred by non-core offshoots. Desperately seeking growth through different buyer types can make separating core from non-core activities challenging. If your company tries to grow too fast, there will be lots of complicated information. Often, leaders make broad assumptions about the market that don't hold upon close examination. For example, you may think your core is "elastic legal services on demand for law firms and companies." However, upon analysis, you realize that you're only consistently successful with small law firms and that large clients are hard to win and not profitable.

A strong core business should satisfy the following criteria:

- **Clear**: While it may be initially challenging to pin down, your core should be evident to most people involved in the company once it's been clarified. Articulating your core succinctly will be crucial to decision-making, as seen later in this chapter.

- **Defensible**: Your differentiation should be sustainably secure. A crowded market or imminent threat of disruption could call that into question. A strong core provides a short- and long-term "moat" of protection and enough market room to support growth goals.

- **Leads easily to other markets**: Many companies get into trouble because they use their success with their initial buyer as justification for growth into markets that are harder to win, have different needs, are more expensive to serve, and are less loyal. A strong core allows you to expand into other markets without a massive effort once you have saturated your initial market.

Ideally, your core business is also aligned with your purpose.

Keeping people motivated on the "why" of their work is critical. To the extent possible, show people how the core business supports the company's larger vision and why it exists.

To uncover your clear, defensible, and sustainable core business, ask yourselves the following questions about your business:

CUSTOMERS:

- Why do customers stay with you? What do they love about you and your offering? How do they describe you?

- What segments of customers do you serve? How profitable is each segment? How unique are the needs of each?

- Have your customers' pain points changed over time? How?

- Is your offering a "must-have" or a "nice-to-have?" What would make it something customers couldn't live without?

SALES:

- Where do you win? Why?

- Where do you lose? Why?

- If you have a sales team, which reps are most effective? Why?

- What sales have you made that caused problems? (Were specific segments unsatisfied or overly expensive to satisfy?)

MARKET:

- How do industry experts perceive you?

- What do competitors think of you? (Sometimes, it's worth calling them and finding out directly from them. It's surprising what insights can be gleaned from a frank call.)

- How might a more innovative player disrupt you?

- What will the market look like in three to five years? What insights or beliefs do you firmly hold about its future?

EMPLOYEES:

- How does the team describe the business? What do they think the company is best at doing? And what vision for the future resonates most strongly?

- What do they think went wrong? (This might shed light on unidentified problem areas.)

- What drives them? What would increase that motivation?

ASSETS:

- What elements of the business are most valuable (knowledge, intellectual property, technology, people, or processes)?

- Do you have a valuable but underutilized asset?

As you answer these questions about your core, remember

you're looking for what you are (or can be) the best in the world at doing—what your customers love and what drives a healthy business. It might be the design of your products compared to alternatives, deep technology expertise, or ironclad relationships with partners. Even small, your core could be the seed of potential greatness. Your description of your core business should include your product and your market. Some sample descriptions:

- The largest professional network for sales executives to advance their careers.

- The industry experts in customer service AI for mid-market, e-commerce companies.

- The leading mobile application for large-chain hotel workers.

- The toughest socks for serious hikers.

- The most reseller-friendly tablet security software.

If you find that your core no longer meets the criteria listed earlier in this section—it's no longer clear, defensible, or sustainable because competitors have caught up, or the market is saturated or dying, or new technology has killed your differentiation—like Chase and QPass, you might need to keep digging until you find a solid foundation.

If there is no core to build from, it may not be worth the effort to transform your company. Trying to change a business with no core is like baking a cake without a pan. There must be an element of unique strength that will dominate a market segment.

The most obvious example of a company rediscovering its core is Apple. In 1997, it was on the verge of bankruptcy when Steve Jobs returned to save it. Jobs had to humbly start his "second coming" by taking on a $150 million investment from Microsoft, formerly Apple's sworn enemy. He recognized that the previous "Microsoft versus Apple" mentality was historical baggage and that Apple's rebirth must come from its essence.

Instead of defining Apple's core business as selling computers for the education and graphic design markets, Jobs took the company down to the studs, down to its founding belief: simple, beautiful design. Apple cut huge parts of its business to refocus its precious few resources on making sexy new products: first, the iMac and iBook in 1998, followed by the iPod in 2001. In the process, they took risks and experienced failures. But Jobs' ravenous focus on design—a return to their core—won the hearts and minds of consumers. Refocusing its efforts on its core transformed Apple into the largest company in the world.

What Is *Not* Your Core?

Equally crucial to defining your core business is clarifying what is *not* core. To do this, you need to understand how the energetic flows of time and effort have driven your company's strategic and financial results. Transformation is contingent on cutting out distractions. Every bit of capital needs to be made available to the core business. Stuck companies are often like a traveler who packed a giant suitcase for a road trip but must now hike up a mountain. You need a finely tuned machine—built for purpose and single-minded in its mission.

To truly identify what is and is *not* your core business, create a whiteboard with your core business in the center. Then list all other initiatives—areas of significant investments such as products, service lines, technology, or innovations you are developing, target markets you are chasing, partnerships or acquisitions you are pursuing—as circles in relation to the core. The more relevant the initiative is to the core, the closer it should be drawn to the center.

Here's a hypothetical example of a core business "map" for a lifestyle clothing brand known for its sweatshirts—its core (see Figure 2.1). Sweatpants, a clothing item the brand is considering, could be closer to the core. The smartphone pockets for its sweatshirts or the sunglasses product line would be further away. In this example, I organized the initiatives into four categories: capabilities, product, innovation, and market. Yours may have different categories.

Once you've completed listing all the initiatives, answer the following questions about each of them:

- **Support of core business:** How much does it directly impact the success of your core business?

- **Competitive advantage:** Related to the above, how critical is this initiative to your company's long-term differentiation and sustainability?

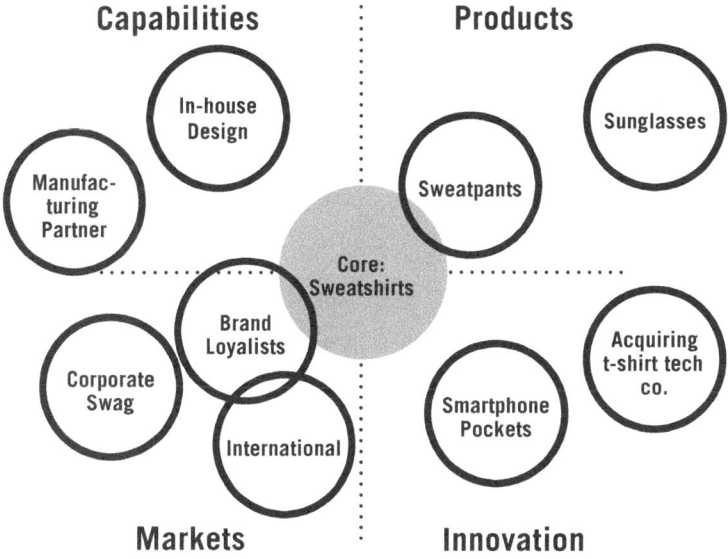

Figure 2.1 Core Business Map

- **Productivity:** How effective is your company at this activity, and how could you do it cheaper, better, or faster than you do today?

- **Capabilities:** How important is it that we source this activity internally?

- **Financial results:** If you can measure the initiative's financial health, what are those results? What is the total spend, revenue, and profit (if that data is available)?

- **Saturation:** If this is a market you're serving, how much room is there to grow and suit the business needs? What is the market size and saturation percentage (if that data is available)?

- **External threats:** Is the long-term health of this initiative threatened by competition with newer technology or an alternative business model?

At this point, the non-core initiatives should start to stand out: Which of them had seemed relevant and promising but have not turned out that way? You should be able to identify the non-core initiatives that are pulling the company into distracting, unfertile territory—areas that don't align with your core business or that, to succeed, need a lot more care and feeding than you have given them so far and will distract from the core business.

Usually, these non-core activities fall into four categories:

- **Required but can be streamlined:** Some non-core activities are critical to the business's health and differentiation. But there is almost always an opportunity for improving their cost and effectiveness. Perhaps they can be done by a partner, by an offshore resource, or with half the number of people.

- **Profitable but unsustainable:** These are the "red herrings" of strategy. They are the business opportunities that appear to be working well but fail to meet the "sustainable" criteria: They either require too much work for the profit they deliver (or assumed profit if it's not an initiative where you can calculate profit directly), or they are in a market where you don't have the advantage. These initiatives distract you from long-term health.

- **Unprofitable and unsustainable:** These initiatives seemed a good idea at some point, but you never turned them into a healthy business. New competitors with better products have entered the market, your sales team isn't hitting their goals, and the customer needs are spreading your resources thin.

- **Experimental:** These are products and customer segments you have been dabbling in but haven't validated as a real market opportunity. Experiments are essential, but when your company is stalled, you must shelve them until the business is healthy. Running experiments is an earned luxury.

Once you've identified core versus non-core, it's time for action. Instead of aiming to become a unicorn, it's time to become a cheetah—a lean, sinewy sprinter with unprecedented focus and reaction time. It's time to win a smaller market decisively. It's time to reorganize around your core.

Reorganize around Your Core

Even multibillion-dollar companies started as focused million-dollar companies. Google had a better search algorithm for websites using a unique PageRank system. Airbnb rented inflatable beds at friends' houses during conferences. Amazon sold books on a website. In each case, there was something inherently better about how they approached the small market they entered that set them apart and made it clear how to expand: for Google, it was better search results, for Airbnb, it was human-centric design, for Amazon, it was the easiest customer experience.

The goal at this stage is to clarify your core—much like Google, Amazon, and Airbnb did once—and then reorganize your business around it. What is the leanest, most effective organizational design for delivering your core business to the world?

Once you know the answer, you can (1) design a new business model, (2) identify the ideal team, and (3) eliminate all non-core activities and people.

1. SKETCH THE NEW BUSINESS MODEL (THE "HOW" AND "WHAT")

After defining your core, it's time to figure out how to best bring that core to the world. The way to do that is to sketch your business model—your strategy for creating value and making money. Your business model may be similar to how your core business is conducted today, but analyzing the moving pieces with fresh eyes is essential. Imagine you were building this company from scratch, focused solely on your core and staying as lean as possible. How would you organize the people, processes, systems, and finances? If you've been with the company for a while, involve advisors, consultants, and friends. Too much experience leads to blind spots. You could miss big areas for improvement.

There are many books on creating business models (such as *Business Model Canvas*), so I won't delve too deeply into the details of the process. A simple way to map your model is to focus on the following:

- **Ideal customer**: Who is the right buyer for your core offering? Which segment will you focus your efforts on? This is where most companies go astray, so be specific and deliberate, avoid using old assumptions about buyers, and ensure you're not defining the buyer too broadly.

- **Value proposition**: How will your new or revised offering be unique and attractive to customers? If you tighten your market focus, can you also tighten your positioning so it better connects to your customers' pain points?

- **Economic engine**: What structure for your business will optimize profitability? What are the keys to freeing enough cash to invest in a thriving core? What is the ideal pricing, packaging, and promotion?

- **Needed resources**: What assets will you need to succeed?

- **Processes**: What processes do you need to own, and what can you outsource? How can the workflows be further optimized to support the core business? What will it look like when it's a well-oiled machine?

The resulting business model, visual or text-based, should be a clean, easy-to-understand (typically one-page) overview of the new, focused business and how it will produce its most profitable output.

2. IDENTIFY THE IDEAL TEAM (THE "WHO")

After creating the business model, you can list the roles required to support the new model and identify who would be ideal to fill those roles.

Effective transformation requires people who are flexible enough to deal with change and strategic enough to build a new infrastructure. It would be best to have fewer "specialists"—who are good in the mature stages of the business—and more "renaissance" players who perform many functions well. You need people who aren't stressed by change but thrive on it. You will be orchestrating a deep immersion into the core business, followed later by thoughtful experimentation for future growth. This process is best served by a figure-it-out energy rather than a scale-it energy in your team.

To build your new, leaner team, follow these steps:

1. **Make a list of your ideal team characteristics**. What other attributes will be important in this phase? What culture do you want to foster? Conversely, what attributes got the company into trouble in the past?

2. **Appraise your current staff**. Gauge your team's overall performance and how well they fit into the new business model and ideal team characteristics. Use past performance reviews to ensure there are no unconscious biases toward individuals. It is hugely problematic for a CEO to surround themselves with "people who look like me," which destroys diversity, creates a toxic culture, generates legal problems, and

can kill the company. The goal is to use clear, consistent, and transparent criteria to put employees into three categories of how well-suited they are for this next phase: great fit, possible fit, or likely not a fit.

3. **Build your ideal org chart.** What would it look like if you could build the business from scratch, focus solely on your core business, and stay as lean as possible? Would you have one exec oversee both sales and customer service to avoid issues? Keep only the salespeople focused on a particular market? No salespeople at all until the product is more stable? Outsource the back-office functions?

4. **Fill in the org chart.** Add your "great fit" employees to their ideal position. Then, see if your "possible fit" employees would thrive in unfilled roles. For any parts that can't be filled with your current team, put To Be Hired (TBH).

5. **Check your thinking.** Once you've done a pass, bring in your HR person, if you have one, and other key advisors and staff. Ensure you are making the right decisions and not falling prey to biases. Are you putting too much emphasis on loyalty? How close are you to the person? Are there any inadvertent issues around age, gender, race, religion, or other personal factors? Deciding whom to keep is fraught with challenges, so don't go into it lightly.

The result should be an org chart with the right people

in the right roles. If you have conducted the process with transparency, consistency, sensitivity, and clarity, the result should be a streamlined, focused, motivated team that can drive change.

How many people you need to fill your chart will depend, of course, on your business, current staff, and the scope of your reinvention. But unless you've already conducted layoffs, there should be fewer people than you have today. I have never regretted cutting deeper than was comfortable. Taking things down to the studs allows you the freedom to invest in what matters.

LUKE KANIES:
SEPARATING CORE FROM NON-CORE

Luke Kanies was the founder, initial developer, and long-time CEO of Puppet, which makes software that automates the application and data infrastructure for companies. In 2015, Luke wrote the code that would become Puppet and ran the company through 2016. Under his leadership, the company raised $87 million, grew beyond 500 employees, and had over 30,000 companies using the software. Eventually, Puppet was acquired by Perforce in 2022. Luke has seen great success but made some mistakes that he graciously shared.

What did you learn about your core business at Puppet?
Looking back now, I can see the big picture. But when you're in it, it's challenging. You can't separate the rational from rationalizing. Raising so much money obfuscated the truth and allowed

us to put off decisions. We didn't understand our core business, which was selling the product we already had to customers who looked like our existing customers. We had a "peanut butter" budgeting strategy (i.e., spread thin across many projects) that looked at the entire business instead of thoughtfully separating the core from new investments. So we struggled with investment decisions: do we improve the product for existing customers, build new products for new customers, or invest in new products for existing customers?

How did that problem manifest?

We didn't know what initiatives and projects were working. Like many growth companies, we had one big P&L that worked at a high level, but the underlying details were obfuscated. For instance, we tried multiple times to build a partnership organization that could drive revenue. But it never worked. It cost money without delivering value, and we realized it too late. We also expanded internationally too quickly, going from one small partner organization in Amsterdam to lots of salespeople on the ground in different countries, with international leaders in two geographies. This was a huge change, required a ton of energy from leadership, and was not managed as the experiment that it was.

How did the team contribute to the problem?

Our people were good, but their skill sets didn't always align with what we needed for our core. For instance, the finance team was great at managing cash and traditional reporting, but they couldn't express the finances through the lens of company strategy, so we couldn't see what worked and how best to invest. Marketing and sales seemed to be working at a high level, but when I dug in on our lead flows and conversion, it became clear

continued

that we had been putting customers into categories that didn't reflect the reality of the buying patterns. I based decisions on a rationalized narrative of who was buying which products for what reasons, only to learn the truth too late. I was too removed from the analysis, and it came back to haunt me.

How do you think about funding a growth business now?
VC is a treadmill you can never get off. We raised once per year for four years, and then 18 months later, we raised again. That was too much. My philosophy is that every 18 months, leaders should do a gut check: stay on the treadmill (raise more money) or get off (get profitable). This should be based on understanding their core business and market opportunity. You want to build a team that will become self-sustaining with your investment, not jump the gun and overinvest based on some idea of the huge company you think you will become.

3. ELIMINATE NON-CORE ACTIVITIES AND POSITIONS

This step is hands-down the most challenging part of the transformation process. You will likely face judgment from colleagues, peers, and others involved with the company for your choices. You will have sleepless nights about it and experience bouts of self-doubt. If you're a founder or long-time leader, you will feel like you let people down. That's the hard truth.

It's tough to say goodbye to people who have been loyal throughout the journey. It's tough to end projects and initiatives that seemed exciting when they were kicked off: a line of business you spent months of your life pulling together, a "Tiger" team working on a new product, or a business development group working to form new partnerships. These initiatives and groups were created with good intentions but have become the organizational plaque that slows the engine down.

Cutting weight and focusing on the core can be one of the most rewarding parts of the journey as you witness the business change into a healthy, lean enterprise. Streamlining can be a cathartic exercise that, after the initial feelings of shock, change, and loss, can bring mojo back as the organization adjusts to its new, lighter, agile body.

But in the moment, it feels awful. Whether it's three people or three hundred, layoffs are always rough. Most of mine have involved tears. But it is necessary to survive. And the employees and leaders who remain must understand and support this transition.

As I write this, I am wrapping up a consulting contract where I had to provide a professional opinion about the best path for a $50 million e-commerce business that kept needing more funding. Frankly, there was no other option than to get profitable, as painful a pill as it was to swallow. No one would fund the business if it wasn't profitable and there were no buyers. It was not a fun result for the weary CEO, but it was the only path. And if you can make it through the process, the other side is much more enjoyable.

I've seen poorly conducted layoffs, where employees feel abandoned, betrayed, and angry with leadership. If leaders don't treat departing people with deep sensitivity and good packages and don't jump in to help the remaining team process the restructure while keeping the communication flowing, the culture can become toxic. But when it's done well, there is no "us versus them" thinking between employees and leaders. Everyone supports getting the business back to health. And you can lead the charge.

No restructuring is perfect, but you can do it professionally and compassionately by following these guidelines:

- **Be transparent**. Overcommunicate and listen. Explain in detail why you are doing the layoff, how hard it was, why you made the decisions you did, and how you handled the process. There can't be any confusion about why the layoffs and restructuring are happening and how you are going about it. And make sure everyone feels heard and valued throughout the process.

- **Do it once**: Cut as deeply as needed in one round instead of laying off swaths of people over time. Drawn-out, intermittent layoffs create anxiety for everyone, making it hard for people to stay focused. Employees dread coming into work wondering if they'll be next.

- **Treat people well**: The lives of those people who are being laid off are changing in dramatic ways. Respect what they are going through and support their process. Be as generous as you can with severance packages. The employees you're keeping are friends with these people. Treat those leaving with deep respect; the people you keep will respect you in return. Conduct one-on-one meetings with the exiting employees. Offer to write

LinkedIn recommendations. Work hard to find them jobs in other companies. Show them you are committed to their journey.

- **Keep people together**: If you work from physical offices, consider consolidating employees onto fewer sites. Or, if you work remotely, set up some weeks in one city where people can work together in person. That proximity will allow people to help each other out through the restructuring. They'll see you and other leadership daily and form the bonds needed to deal with the change.

- **Establish a new world order**: Before the restructuring, mistakes led to these layoffs. If you were in charge then, own those mistakes. Admit what went wrong and explain why it won't happen again. Your people need to trust you and your leadership more than ever.

- **Stay connected**: Schedule all-hands meetings and invite questions and discussion after the layoff. Promote open communication—mistrust during this phase will kill your transformation plans. If your company has conducted layoffs in the past, people will be cynical about this "latest round" of changes. Show them this time is different: There's a new mission, a new plan with which they will be intimately involved, and ideally, more money coming in than going out.

After the restructuring, there may be some blowback. There might be hard feelings and people airing grievances on

Glassdoor. There's nothing you can do about that. It's part of the process and will go away over time. But if you restructure compassionately and professionally and keep the right people, your team will rise to the occasion and do it eagerly, with pride, and with a new sense of community. In the next chapter, I'll discuss how to manage post-restructure in more detail.

A Second Chance

All great companies have near-death experiences. It's how they deal with them that matters. Reorganizing around your core is a chance to sandblast the corrosion in your business that has led to it stalling and to get back to your essence. It's about giving your company a second chance to find its greatness by organizing the resources for maximum effect. An opportunity to reframe how the company behaves and what it means to show up for each other every day. A chance to decide how you want things to change and live that change with action. Refocusing on your core will be uncomfortable at times, but it will be real. How *you* handle this moment will symbolize how the company will act in this next phase.

Hard Lessons

In 2007, Jive was doing well. We had been focused on selling our collaboration software to smaller businesses using a lightweight sales process. After raising our first venture capital round of $15 million at Jive, we decided to go up-market and sell to enterprise customers. The competition was frothy at the low end of the market with lots of new vendors. So, we decided that faster growth would come from becoming the only "enterprise-ready" startup to compete against prominent vendors like Microsoft and IBM.

The shift to large companies required significant changes: a new executive team, new sales and marketing teams, a new strategy, and a roadmap focused on large company needs like security, scalability, customization, and complex integration. I didn't realize it then, but we were shifting our core.

So when the sales team came to me wanting to sell to the small businesses that had been our core customers of the past, it sounded reasonable. We still had many leads from that part of the market, and I, applying greedy thinking, thought, "Let's do it! We could own the *whole* market." So, I hired several down-market salespeople and tried to grow across several fronts.

But this move confused our teams and customers. How should we position the product? What features should we prioritize? How should we deliver the product: simple self-service or lots of customization and integration options? What kind of services did small companies need compared to enterprise buyers?

The challenges quickly became apparent: We were no longer set up well to sell to small business customers and couldn't keep them happy if they did purchase our new product. Competitors who focused on small companies were easier and cheaper than us. We wasted time, money, and energy trying to cover the entire market instead of focusing on our new core. Sadly, some of those decisions stayed with the company even after my time, creating long-term priority confusion and slowing the business.

Like a traveler who packed a giant suitcase to hike up a mountain, we were weighed down by distracting non-core activities that took precious funds away from what we needed to survive. I had to learn how to lighten the load and become a finely tuned machine, created for purpose and single-minded in its mission.

CHAPTER 4

Focus Your Team— Building a Healthier, Stable Organization

It's not enough to be busy; so are the ants.
The question is: What are we busy about?

—HENRY DAVID THOREAU

Kristy Gannon was the first employee hired at Fluxx in 2012. Ten years later, she became its CEO, orchestrating a needed business transformation. Her story is a masterclass on how to manage change after getting stuck.

In the early days, Fluxx, which created grants management software for private foundations, was bootstrapped. Drawn to its mission, Kristy joined as the first product leader. She soon learned that the company's scrappy culture was great for financial discipline and focus, but the stress of making payroll would lead to unfortunate trade-offs of cash for innovation. The company would agree to custom projects to win deals and generate revenue, leading to a complicated product with customers on different versions.

Lured by the prospect of building a unicorn and winning its category, the company raised an A round to create new products and capitalize on the data from its core offering. Shortly after, they raised a B round to keep the momentum going.

It soon became apparent that they had overestimated the market size and potential. Additionally, they were writing custom code for individual customers to support unique feature requests, which made innovation challenging because they had to support these customers with unique versions of the product. But the investors wanted more growth. So, the company kept signing these bespoke deals that sacrificed the long-term interest of the company. They were burning cash, slowing their progress, and not building the unicorn they had hoped for.

To stop the bleeding, the board hired a new CEO, Madeline Duva, in 2017. She shifted the organization toward being customer- and team-focused while reorganizing it for profitability. Kristy moved into the COO role to ensure tight operations, clear metrics, and accountability. Fluxx was finally profitable and had a realistic plan, but its meager growth rate of 13 percent no longer matched investor expectations. Madeline, Kristy, and the rest of the leadership team knew they had a strong core business, generating $13 million of recurring revenue with strong retention, but they didn't have the proper investors or capitalization structure to build the business they wanted to create. They were stuck.

My partner at Metamorph, Bob Tinker, acquired Fluxx in April of 2021, becoming its chairman, while Kristy became its CEO, having been mentored by Madeline for years to take on the role. Bob and Kristy aimed to build a healthy, sustainable business around four critical pillars: reasonable growth expectations, customer-led expansion from the core business, product-led reengineering and focus for long-term scale, and a solid culture to deliver on the new mission.

Focusing on its core meant selling off a beloved but underperforming non-core product, which was hard for the team but the right thing to do. It set the tone for the transition. It also meant building a stronger GTM around the core (becoming "the world leader in end-to-end grants management systems") and thoughtfully moving into the next vertical instead of forcing it. Most importantly, it meant organizing the company around these changes.

At first, there was skepticism in the ranks. Kristy was steering away from the old culture, and she needed support. "We didn't have the right leaders for transformation," she told me. "People had grown up in the slow-moving world of philanthropy and were scared to make decisions." Kristy rebuilt the leadership team over the next year with people befitting this stage: people who were unafraid to ask hard questions, unlearn old ways of doing things, and implement needed changes.

She and her new execs introduced a new operating system for the business—new approaches to managing, communicating, and measuring success. For example, one of their significant challenges was that people didn't feel comfortable making decisions. So they instituted "short loops," an approach to making (and celebrating) intelligent, quick decisions throughout the company. The most impactful change they made was focusing more intensely on cross-functional initiatives. The organization previously spent too much energy on functional operations and little time on the "interlocks" across departments. Kristy and the team flipped the model on its head, making significant, cross-functional initiatives paramount, profoundly altering the company's ability to communicate and deliver.

"Consistent, frequent communication is critical," Kristy says about managing post-restructure. "Have all-hands meetings where you reiterate the mission and goals—in our case, the Four Pillars—and lots of AMA (ask me anything) channels for people to ask hard questions." She points to Conway's Law (which states that organizations design systems that mirror their communication structure) as a helpful tool that helped her refocus her team. "Our systems mirrored the complicated ways we had designed the product, killing our productivity," she explains. "We had to recognize that issue and rebuild with scale in mind. Once we had the complete view of the system and all its flaws, our path became clear."

Managing for Health and Stability

Transformation requires a new management system with more focus on clarity, details, and alignment. As the dust settles from your restructuring, rethink how to organize your business—from purpose and strategy down to communication flows, priorities, and metrics—to help the company heal and feel a sense of winning.

It's like your business is going on a car trip from New York to Los Angeles. You need to plan not only the route you're going to take but also where you will stop for gas, how much money you can spend to get there, how long it will take, and what each person is responsible for managing to ensure the trip goes smoothly. In stuck companies, departments operate like different cars (and helicopters, bicycles, and boats) going to different locations on their own timeframes and budgets. This is the time to be in the same vehicle, connected, aligned, and probably singing road trip songs together.

As you think through the changes you need to make, consider the management issues that plagued the company in the past and how you can remedy them moving forward. You can now establish a new set of operating principles and make up for past mistakes, which might include—

- An ill-defined, vague, or self-aggrandizing purpose

- Too many or constantly changing priorities or goals

- Poor sense of market dynamics

- Poor understanding of the core business

- Combining core activities with non-core

- Overly rigid management that leaves little room for agility

- Poor communication of strategy

- Departments operating independently or with little cross-functional collaboration
- Scant celebration of significant wins

If done well and with a strong sense of your core business, achieving clarity in your strategy can be straightforward. Now is the time to be transparent with the team on your core business, how you will exploit it, and how to know when it's working.

Rather than repeat the standard management activities described in many business books, such as setting a vision, mission, and OKRs, I have outlined three management focus areas that are especially helpful in creating a healthy, stable, newly restructured company.

Revive Your Team's Focus and Spirit

Coretta Scott King once said that "the greatness of a community is most accurately measured by the compassionate actions of its members." The same could be said for companies, especially after restructuring. Transitions are complex, requiring a delicate balance of recognizing the difficulties inherent in the change while establishing a new, highly collaborative working style. Starting from the top, people must put aside selfish interests and work toward the larger vision. These are the management approaches that I found to be most important at this stage of the transformation:

- **Be seen.** When leaders show up, others follow. Selfless acts start at the top. Model the collaboration you need at this stage. Don't see tasks as "below you" after the restructure. Jump in to help people with reports, presentations, and accounting cleanup. Give up your budget to help others. If you have an office, pick people up and drive them there. Stay late to help colleagues finish a project. Establish a culture of giving up your needs for the sake of the larger mission.

- **Be transparent.** Early in my career, I would withhold information from my team to present a rosy picture. I was scared people would leave if they learned about the warts and shortcomings. I was wrong. Instead, people felt ownership when I involved them in problems. Show your team the plans, the wins, and the losses. Be vulnerable about your mistakes and shortcomings and how you plan to overcome them.

- **Set achievable goals.** Start with small wins to get the blood flowing and remind people what winning feels like. A "quick win" offers a nice boost after a restructuring and builds confidence across the team. This could be getting profitable, launching a new product, closing a big deal, or instituting a major process improvement in a problem area. Ideally, it's a victory that aligns with the new lean culture and is meaningful across the company. If you set stretch goals, make it clear they are a stretch. Showing progress against reasonable goals gets the blood flowing again, so you don't want too many stretch goals during this "healing" phase.

- **Celebrate your people.** Keep your new team energized and on track. Find ways to thank them for their hard work, collaboration, and "going the extra mile" to support the business. Give out "Home Run" baseballs or ramen noodle packages to save money. Make people feel seen, heard, and valued. As the CEO at Mobilize, I added a "shout-outs" section to our all-hands meeting where people could thank other team members for their excellent work. It became a cultural boost for the company.

- **Combine the old with the new.** Your employees likely have a connection to the company's history. Pay homage to that history while recognizing that things must change. Celebrate the values that helped the company succeed and find ways to keep that initial spirit alive, whether it's fun get-togethers, old traditions, or even unique ways the company operated and innovated.

- **Promote collaboration.** Depending on the size of your company, siloes may have developed, creating pain and confusion. This is the time to own those negative patterns and build connective tissue across the organization. Find opportunities to have people work cross-functionally on visible, meaningful projects like a new all-hands meeting format, a new website project, or a customer advisory group.

- **Check-in frequently.** Stop talking and ask open-ended questions of your team: "How are you doing? Last time we talked, you were dealing with [insert issue]—how is that going? What's the one thing we can be doing better as a company? What big opportunity are we missing?" See how they're doing personally. The bonding during this period will be fuel for the long run.

- **Align compensation models.** Ensure that your people are recognized for the results that drive your transformation. If your company is focused on profitability over the long run, create a profit-sharing plan. If it's company value creation, create a meaningful equity plan where employees can make good money with the anticipated value at exit. Set up bonuses for team members for achievements that directly impact the strategy. This sounds intuitive, but keeping old compensation models without thoroughly evaluating their relevance in the new era is common.

- **Hire new people slowly.** Eventually, you'll need to hire people to support growth. But first, run with a lean team of old employees and any new hires required to keep the core business running. Take time to settle into the new world order. Bring in new people only when there's a shared understanding of why that role is essential. Too much change at once can have adverse effects, and if you bring new leadership in too soon, employees may associate those new executives with layoff decisions. Run lean, even if it's stretching people until it's organizationally urgent (e.g., you have no one running sales), and financially viable to bring on more resources.

- **Involve customers and partners**. Explain your new vision for the company to customers and partners and ask for their insights. Not only does this give you great information for your strategy, but it's also a great time to let them vent. Own any mistakes that affected them and use the connection to strengthen the relationship while making them feel a part of the process.

A clear, core-focused business model and a small team of committed people is a powerful force. A sizeable restructure may shock the system, but a focused, driven culture will emerge faster than you think. I've always been surprised by how quickly people unite when they believe in the mission and team.

This was the case at Bio Products Laboratory (BPL), a dying British governmental healthcare organization that my friend John Perkins was tasked with transforming into a thriving private entity. BPL is hardly a startup, but even a large, mature organization requires similar cultural shifts after a restructuring.

BPL's purpose was inspiring: The organization's business was to extract proteins from human plasma to combat bleeding disorders and immune deficiencies. The organization itself, however, was a disaster. Years of neglect and underinvestment had led to declining revenues, cash burn, a decrepit 30-year-old plant, and a large team that did not believe things could change. "Most people see the glass as half full or half empty," John told me. "These 1,800 bureaucrats couldn't even see a glass." But John pulled off the unimaginable using the levers of change discussed earlier.

After hundreds of conversations with workers, it became clear the plant was the biggest problem. It was on a seemingly endless decline, so John brought on a high-profile COO to rebuild. After a month of assessment, she gave it a 1–2 out of 10 rating. Only a month later, she walked into John's office to inform him that the plant was on fire. "We had to laugh; otherwise we'd be crying," John recalled.

John and the COO put everything they had into modernizing the plant. Not only was this required for the turnaround, but it gave them a win with the team. The employees, especially the old guard, were stunned. The move solidified their belief in the new direction and leadership.

While John brought a needed injection of operational excellence, he sought to maintain a connection to the organization's historical heart and soul. He identified a set of employee skills that represented the old and new values of the organization and evaluated everyone along these lines to determine who was a good fit. He also brought back some old traditions, like the long-dormant company picnic that had been killed years before for cost-saving reasons.

He assembled a global leadership team to drive change through cross-functional cooperation and break through the historically siloed organization. One-third of this new leadership team were long-time employees, one-third were executives John had worked with before, and one-third were new hires. He even brought coaches to help the teams collaborate and work more closely.

John also rebuilt the bonus structure to promote performance across the organization and gave equity to the leadership team to make them feel like owner-operators, which was an entirely new concept to many of them.

Over time, even the most skeptical line employees on the plant floor became believers. The company had a spring in its step. They built a new US operation. Sales doubled. They then doubled again. Profitability followed. They created new jobs and grew to 2,800 people. Most importantly, they improved the lives of people around the world. The turnaround came down to a renewed focus on the core, preserving a connection to the old while bringing new discipline to the execution and ensuring deep alignment and conviction across the organization.

Document — and Share — Your Plan

After restructuring, keeping the energy up and the team organized is vital. I've never met a CEO who said they communicated their transformation plan *too* much. They are almost always surprised by how much they must repeat it. It's not that people aren't smart; they just infer their conclusions from off-hand comments and turn them into narratives that often are at odds with what's going on—or should be going on. A CEO may say, "Future growth should come from government customers," meaning only that the company will test the waters on selling to the government over the following years. Employees may hear that the company is switching its focus to targeting government customers and ditch their plans that support current customers.

The best way to battle miscommunication is to summarize

the critical strategy elements of your transformation into a "one-page plan" and share it widely throughout the company. This living document should leave little room for confusion among your team. When leading a transformation, I like to publish the plan and then update it every quarter. Here's what I include:

- **Why we're doing this (purpose):** The North Star of your business. Why you exist. You never "achieve" your purpose, but rather, you always move in its direction. *Example*: "Improving access to healthcare for all Americans."

- **How we act now (values):** The belief system that guides decision-making for the restructured company. *Example*: "We are customer-obsessed—we see customers not as 'deals' but living, breathing people whose lives we can change for the better."

- **What we need to learn (hypotheses):** The basis of your growth potential. What hypothesis do you need to test to build a breakaway growth strategy? *Example*: "We believe that our gluten-free snacks are unique and loved enough that we can shift from private label to our own direct-to-consumer business in two years."

- **What's important now (priorities and goals):** The annual and quarterly planning done in support of the larger goals, including OKRs and other company metrics. *Example*: "Objective: Expand into the insurance sector. Key Result: Win three new insurance customers in Q2."

In the next chapter, we'll discuss finding your breakaway move—a strategy that drives growth. When the business is healthy and stable, and you can start that process of figuring out what's next, you'll add three more items to the one-page plan: Where the world is headed (worldview), where we're headed (mission), and how we will win (strategy). If you already know how you plan to grow the business in the future, you can consider these items now:

Where the world is headed (worldview): How the world will change and how you are uniquely suited to enable that change given your purpose and core. *Example*: "The rise of autonomous vehicles will drive a need for our innovative road beacon technology that combines human design with AI and data collection, and which will help end driving fatalities."

Where we're headed (mission): Your five- to ten-year goal, which represents the change you are seeking in the world or is an indication that the change has occurred. *Example*: "Over 10 million people around the world will rely on our electric scooters for transportation."

How we will win (strategy): Your plan of attack used to achieve your mission. It describes how you will execute on your chosen path. *Example*: "We will win the mid-sized consumer goods manufacturer market with the only modern, data-driven accounting application in the market, after which we will move up-market to the largest manufacturers."

Having everything from why you exist to what is most important right now on one well-considered page is a symbol of strategic clarity. Your team should understand and be fired up to do the needed work. The one-page plan is the constitution of your new world order.

VICTOR CHO: ORGANIZING FOR EXCELLENCE THROUGH TRANSITION

Victor knows how to organize teams after a restructuring. He has seen it all and understands that success is not a whiteboard exercise, but a human endeavor. After working for companies like Microsoft, Intuit, and Kodak (during its restructure), Victor ran multiple companies with successful exits. He was the CEO of Evite after successfully buying and rebuilding the company for seven years. He was then on the board for a couple of years and recently stepped down (still an equity owner) to focus on his new startup. Victor's passion for building high-scale, market-defining online customer experiences is evident. But what I find most compelling is the management path he takes to get there: transparency, empathy, diversity, and integrity.

What's the best way to go through a restructure?
First and foremost, you need a strong thesis on your strategy. Just cutting costs will likely remove people who are critical for the path you end up pursuing, so you need to know what mountain you're climbing first. Second, people don't cut as deeply as they should. That's why outside CEOs do well in these situations: Existing leaders know too much about the risks. For a restructure, you must put the business into a risky state to free up the capital needed to pursue the next thing. The third would be that you can't be too optimistic. Kodak was a great example: They had a good thesis for getting into the printing business and had the

continued

best execs for the job. But they didn't cut far enough and overestimated how fast they could scale. You must be brutally realistic about what you can achieve in what timeframe.

How do you help people go through the change?
My approach is to go "clean slate." Everyone must forget the company that was and understand that this is a ground-up rebuild around a new strategy, priorities, and operating structure. And I do it all very transparently. I have never been bitten by hypertransparency. People are rational, and, while they may not agree with all the decisions, you have their trust. They've been through a lot, and that trust is paramount. By involving the team in the process, you will see which people can shed the past and work well in the new world order. For some people, it will be hard emotionally, and they will not enjoy the ride. The kindest thing you can do is to let them go, and you can do it with empathy.

How do you organize people around the new mission?
Once you have a strategic roadmap, you can set cascading goals that ripple down into the teams. Everyone needs to see how they are contributing to the mission. At each level, we have an OKR with a success metric and timeline and clear alignment to the organizational priorities. Each team can then present their priorities. If those priorities don't seem to be synced, the execs can figure out a path to reconcile the issue.

How does "The Fourth Stakeholder" factor into your management style?
I first came across stakeholder capitalism—the idea that companies need to focus on other stakeholders besides shareholders, primarily employees and customers—while working at Microsoft and Intuit. It's a wonderful way to hold businesses

and people accountable. If you are an exec who has achieved a modicum of success, you have a responsibility to give back to society. No one does anything that's not built on the shoulders of others. So I codified the Fourth Stakeholder into a set of management principles. Not only is factoring it in the right thing to do, but increasingly important if you want to stay relevant with younger generations.

Don't Rush to Grow

What does a strong core business look like? When are you healthy and stable enough to start experimenting with growth opportunities? Although a "healthy" core business will look different for each company, it will likely fall into a sweet spot between profits and growth (see Figure 3.1).

Ideally, you want more money coming in than going out, with enough growth in your core market to maintain energy among the team. Too much growth usually comes at a high cost and can affect profitability, so it's rare to have high growth and high profits for any company, much less one going through a transformation. And if growth is too high, it will likely stress a lean team. What you're trying to do is get enough organizational and financial stability that you can dedicate resources, people, and attention on assessing and identifying the ideal future strategy.

After this phase of the transformation, you want a calm, moderately predictable business. You're in the liminal space between the old, stuck business and the new, "to-be-determined"

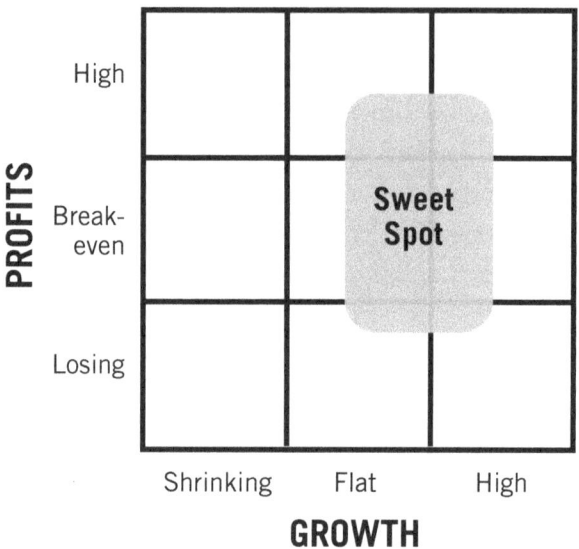

Figure 3.1 Profits and Growth Sweet Spot

growth business. The most important part of this phase is not jumping into new areas too quickly, as it will likely cause confusion and lead to getting even more stuck.

Hard Lessons

Monsoon was a dying company. Its core business was helping businesses that sold books, CDs, and DVDs to sell their products on e-commerce marketplaces like Amazon and eBay. And it was suffering for good reason: Physical media was a hot market in 2005. Not so much in 2017, when most media had been digitized.

After a failed merger, Monsoon's private equity (PE) owners

hadn't done anything with the company for years. Its product had stagnated, the team was demoralized, and customers hadn't heard anything from its leaders in years. Revenue went from $10 million to $5 million over two years and was shrinking fast. When I bought and took over—my first acquisition on my own—revenue was around $4 million and shrinking at 37 percent per year. I like a challenge. But I still had a lot to learn.

When I became CEO, I was clear with my team: The business was in dire straits and needed saving. I zeroed in on the core business. I called all the customers to listen to their challenges and do a "diving catch" to keep them. Soon, I got a sense of the market and could see where the floor was—the natural point was $3 million, a point where we could stabilize the business if we focused on keeping our customers successful and happy.

But instead of cutting the weight and streamlining around the core, I hired a salesperson to improve the top line. Then I brought a new technology from a previous company I worked with that was wildly different from what Monsoon had sold before. The new product didn't make sense for the business, and customers didn't understand our strategy. The salesperson couldn't land any deals. The revenue was still shrinking while I was *adding* expenses.

Rather than being the ruthless operator the business needed, I was the overly excited entrepreneur looking for growth everywhere and trying to force it on a company that wasn't ready. The team didn't have time to heal from the change. I was running an overly ambitious strategy that the team couldn't execute. I hadn't earned the right to invest in growth because I hadn't fully stabilized the business. I came in guns blazing, but all I did was add confusion to an already hard situation.

Recognizing my mistake, I finally acted. I streamlined the Portland, Oregon-based team from twenty-four to seven, treating the laid-off people well on the way out. I cut the new product and the salespeople I had brought in to support it. I moved core engineering to a team in India that knew the product. And I spent more time with existing customers.

For the next year, we focused on stability. We stopped the bleeding and got the business to a place where it wasn't shrinking. We even added customers here and there. It was highly profitable and stable. The team was happy. I brought on a talented operational CEO to run the operations. From there, we could patiently investigate growth opportunities, but if nothing appeared, continue to run the company profitably.

My lesson was how important it is to embrace stability and predictability—and not rush to expand—until the company is truly ready. Think of this "limbo phase" as a chance not only to heal but to feel the pull of future opportunities instead of forcing them on the market. Getting to this state is a lot of work, so I learned how to celebrate the accomplishment and not race toward the next thing.

CHAPTER 5

Evaluate Growth Thoughtfully— Find Your Breakaway Move Without Getting Re-Stuck

Sooner or later, something seems to call us onto
a particular path . . . this is what I must do, this
is what I've got to have. This is who I am.

—JAMES HILLMAN

Russ Heddleston, Dave Koslow, and Tony Cassanego founded DocSend in 2013. With a few million in seed funding, they built a product that allowed people to share documents as links instead of attachments and track what people did with those documents.

Initially launched as a free product, it was a hit with users. They tapped into a big pain point around sharing files, and their well-executed, self-service flows made it simple for customers to get the product up and running. The idea was to become a ubiquitous platform before they started adding the paid editions of the product. That would also give them time to figure out the most promising use cases that could drive their growth.

Some of the most exciting buyers of the product were sales organizations, who used the free product to send presentations, proposals, and other documents to potential buyers. It was a massive market with big budgets. Early traction with this customer base indicated DocSend could succeed. Seeing this opportunity, Russ, Dave, and Tony raised an $8 million Series A round to go after sales enablement buyers.

Going after this market proved more challenging than expected, however. While DocSend had a good product, it wasn't purpose-built for sales enablement like other offerings. It was missing enterprise features the economic buyer (the person with the authority to write the check) needed. Other companies, already entrenched in the sales enablement space, were raising hundreds of millions in venture financing. This meant DocSend had to fight for every sale they made and couldn't close the competitive gap.

After three years, they had only gotten to $4 million in revenue—not the "hockey stick" growth curve investors wanted—and half of that was from their self-service product. "We were built for end users, not economic buyers," said Russ.

"Competing in that space was like playing a golf tournament with clubs half the normal size." They couldn't raise more money and were spending what cash they had on an expensive sales and marketing organization.

Feeling the runway getting shorter, a frustrated Russ made a couple of moves. He trimmed the staff to focus more on the company's core and paused hiring until revenue caught up to expenses. In parallel, he launched what he called "Project Couch Change." The idea was to find minor improvements in their offering that could drive a $50,000 lift in DocSend's annual revenue. While it was a modest amount of revenue, the hope was that these experimental improvements would illuminate the path to a new DocSend strategy and a future for the company.

Russ, along with the director of strategy, Bryan Gaertner, and several team members with intimate knowledge of customer usage, interviewed customers about how they used the product and why they loved it. They learned that buyers of the lower editions needed only a few additional features to be convinced to upgrade to the more expensive option. Customers even told them they weren't charging enough— that their low price point raised concerns that the product might be missing key security features. Most importantly, they learned that if a buyer's needs were external (sending outside their organization), custom (a presentation created specifically for who it was sent to), critical, and sensitive, it was a slam dunk for DocSend to win their business.

With these clear and actionable insights, Russ and the team made significant product changes. First, they killed off the limited, free-forever offering in favor of a two-week trial, as it was cannibalizing their sales efforts and not contributing to lead flow. They created three editions or plans: Personal (for founders and small and midsize businesses), Standard (for sales users), and Finance (for people who cared about security) to reflect buyers' needs better. They made almost all of the products self-service and put all pricing on the site to optimize the buyer flows.

The results were incredible. Buyers loved the new, high-end "Finance Edition" as it gave them the security and compliance features and peace of mind they needed. It was so popular that only 30 percent of customers who bought this edition were in the finance industry. It had far broader appeal than expected, which led to its being renamed "Advanced Plan." In addition, the conversion rates to acquire and upgrade customers were climbing quickly. Within a few months, they had beaten their Project Couch Change goal by 10X. This meant they had $500,000 of new revenue and a clear path to their breakout play and the rebirth of the new DocSend.

With growth back on track and a robust and focused engine supporting that growth, VCs came knocking, and DocSend soon had a $20 million term sheet. But instead of accepting the biggest check, Russ did something most entrepreneurs have a hard time doing: He took only $5 million of financing. This was the amount he needed to feel secure in building a healthy, lean, disciplined business around the new strategy.

The business broke even at $5 million in revenue, and Russ and his team never had to touch the $5 million of venture money. Because of DocSend's strong core business, they no longer needed to invest in paid advertising, just word of mouth and content marketing. They tripled the business in a few years to over $13 million in annual recurring revenue (ARR), at which point Dropbox came knocking. Dropbox acquired DocSend in 2021 for $165 million—a roughly 13X revenue multiple. Dropbox has continued to invest in DocSend and has made it a key part of its strategy to "help customers across industries manage end-to-end document workflows."[6]

Investigating Breakaway Strategies

Once your business is stable and healthy, you have the time and space to investigate possible breakaway strategies.

Breakaway Strategy: A market-validated "go big" strategy that promotes fast growth and unfair advantage inside a large market.

Identifying a breakaway strategy feels daunting even to a brand-new company—much more so to a company in recovery. But when done well, it can create massive value by igniting growth, motivating employees, and reframing customer conversations. Without a stable core, finding a breakaway move creates confusion and urgency that compromises sound decision-making.

---

6   "Dropbox Announces Fourth Quarter and Fiscal 2022 Results," investors.dropbox.com, February 16, 2023, https://investors.dropbox.com/static-files/063f9439-f3a8-4de0-8c69-06017c029b86.

The trick to finding your breakaway move during a company transformation is to connect your core—almost always focused on a small market segment—to a much larger opportunity. There are five steps to finding your breakaway move: assemble the team, collect and analyze information, articulate your hypotheses, test your hypotheses, and choose a strategic move . . . or wait. While many books explain the process of finding growth in startups, I will focus on the methods that work well in a newly transformed company. Specifically, my approach is about being patient, connecting that breakaway move to your core strength, and being open to many potential outcomes, including not finding a breakaway move.

1. ASSEMBLE THE TEAM

In Chapter 1, I discussed the types of people best suited for each stage of a company's lifecycle (page 23). When figuring out your breakaway move, you'll need to assemble a team of people who have the attributes of both Stage 1 and Stage 2 of the company life cycle. This means a combination of the creative, mission-driven, chaos-embracing product builders who can get a company off the ground and the scrappy, collaborative business-builders who understand the infrastructure needed to support a new strategy.

Like DocSend's Couch Change team, you want people who can align big product ideas with market needs and have experience with the realities of the market. In short, innovators and org-builders. If you could see the members of this team starting their own companies, you are on the right track. Entrepreneurial traits are welcome.

The right team is also small—ideally three to five—and covers a broad set of product, market, and internal organization skills and expertise. All members of the team should be able to:

- **Think big and small:** Strategic decisions must be grounded in reality while setting the company up for high growth. You want people who can see the bigger picture of the market and the intricacies of your core business.

- **Be open to new ideas:** Your team members must be good at coming up with ideas and be receptive to others' opinions. Find colleagues who "seek to understand before being understood": people who are good at listening and embrace a "Yes and . . ." mentality that improves upon others' ideas.

- **Remain enthusiastic:** Finding your breakaway move can be a long process. Recruiting people with marathon energy who can keep teammates excited throughout the process is best. They lie awake at night brainstorming ideas and text you over the weekend to share them.

- **Diverse:** Often, CEOs can unknowingly surround themselves with people who think like them and don't question the CEO's judgment. This form of narcissism will kill the company if not handled early and thoroughly. This team is no exception. It should be diverse in backgrounds and experience but also reflect the world and buyer profiles in which the company will likely operate.

Similarly, your strategy team should have the following areas represented:

- **Market:** Someone with a deep sense of the larger market you operate in—the competition, buying drivers, trends, and forces at play. Ideally, this person also understands the "big story" and the opportunity to emerge as unique in the market.

- **Product:** Someone who understands the inner workings of your core product, technology trends, and what's possible to create.

- **Buyer:** Someone who lives in the field and understands customer pain points and how the product or service is woven into their lives.

- **Team:** Ensure that employees and organizational structure are represented so you don't make faulty assumptions or decisions about how the company would be organized to deliver on the idea.

- **Process:** Someone who is excellent at driving decision-making and progress. This person ensures that the strategy work doesn't stay in the ivory tower but becomes clear action plans with metrics to track against those plans.

Pulling together the right team is more complicated than it sounds. Almost everyone loves working on "the new thing." (Search your LinkedIn connections for "strategy" to see what I mean.) But not everyone is excellent at it. This is a chance to not just pick the "usual suspects" from your executive team but to honestly think through a diverse, talented, creative team that could pull off magic together. Take your time and possibly even interview people. The composition of this team has enormous repercussions on your long-term success.

2. COLLECT AND ANALYZE INFORMATION

Once you have a team, the next step is to amass a treasure trove of data to inform your strategic hypotheses. The more extensive your research, the more likely you will find a breakaway move. It's like learning chords on a guitar before figuring out how to play a song. Here's how to go about it:

- **Get the team's perspective.** Meet with key employees one-on-one to understand their thoughts on the company's future and their past experiences with what worked and what didn't. Ask them, "What do you think we should do?" Look for patterns: What motivates them? What beliefs do they share that could fuel future performance (e.g., "We have always been beloved for our great customer service; I don't want to lose that.")? Do they suffer "team PTSD" from previous failures? From these conversations, try to understand better what strategies (or elements of the strategies) excite employees.

- **Review historical decisions and experiments**. Review the strategic moves that were considered, researched, and tried before the company became stuck. Then ask why these potential strategic moves did (or did not) amount to anything. Do any of them represent a possible future? Can you pick up where these were left off on the validation process? Whether you have been with the company since its inception or joined more recently, review old research and data with a clinical eye to see what can be learned from the past.

- **Create a market map**. Research your competitors through analyst reports, industry experts, press, customers, and, if possible, the competitors themselves to understand the market landscape you are operating in. What vectors are other players competing on? What are the sacred, immovable parts of your competitors' strategies? How nimble is each player? How many investors are involved, and what is the approach of those investors (e.g., a competitor may be owned by a PE firm that runs businesses to maximize profits over growth)? How do those competitors view your company in the market? Then, collect intelligence on adjacent market categories' current and potential future states.

- **Analyze the strengths of your core business**. Study the most significant advantages of your core offering. How can you use the unique strength of your core offering to address a larger market and scope of offering? Your core is like the seed of a great oak tree—your potential is written into its DNA, but it needs the right time, space, and environment to flourish. The more you know about that unique DNA, the closer you are to finding your breakaway move.

- **Review industry and technology trends.** Identify the trends that have already peaked and those that have the potential to reshape the category you compete in. What trends are competitors following? What topics are beaten to death at trade shows? What trends are closest to your core and might enable future growth strategies? Look at what's happening in adjacent and analogous industries, as well. Are there comparable companies building market share using new technology, business models, partnerships, or other breakaway strategies?

After collecting and analyzing the data and information, develop several ideas for where the business can head. You might already have a working assumption or an intuitive sense of what growth strategy to pursue. But before jumping to a conclusion, however, you need to vet these ideas.

3. ARTICULATE YOUR HYPOTHESES

As leaders, we often fall in love with big ideas and either act on them too quickly (i.e., we are overly gut-driven) or have difficulty taking action (i.e., we are overly slow and data-driven). The better path is likely in the middle of those two extremes.

Since we often operate with limited data and a constantly changing environment, we must work from hypotheses. A *hypothesis* is a supposition that something is true. It is not entirely provable but represents higher-level reasoning you can use to act. Testing your hypotheses will allow you to pursue bold, market-shifting strategies backed by data, and garner the full support of the team that will execute them.

Start by developing three to five strategic hypotheses of what could drive growth in your company. Each hypothesis will represent a different strategy. Here are some examples:

- "Building a white-glove managed service offering around our AI-driven tax forecasting service will allow us to sell to Global 2000 customers."

- "With new clothing trends changing weekly, customers will pay good money for dynamic, daily fashion offerings modeled after celebrity outfits."

- "By adding new large language models and workflows to our AI chat solution, we will be able to expand beyond financial services and into the insurance industry."

- "Law firms who use our document management application would prefer to purchase secure client-collaboration portals from us because of the tight integration of the two products, which would create meaningful differentiation and allow us to move up-market to larger firms."

List your hypotheses on one document. For each possible direction, capture the following:

HOW YOU WILL TEST THAT HYPOTHESIS:

- What interviews do you need to conduct (e.g., existing customers, industry experts, potential customers, partners)?

- What knowledge is required (e.g., "become conversant in blockchain")?

- Which team members will be helpful to the validation process (e.g., "The director of customer implementations has the richest, most up-to-date information on customer use cases.")?

- What strategic questions must you answer (e.g., "Is it better to acquire a company or build our product?")?

THE IMPLICATION OF EACH MOVE:

- Cost of the strategy and source of funding (e.g., "Going after community banks will require $5 million in new funding from a growth PE firm who makes minority investments.")

- Critical roles needed (e.g., "This move would require hiring a well-connected thought leader in brand marketing for large companies.")

- Milestones to hit (e.g., "Reach go/no-go decision by the end of Q2.")

- Valuation impact for shareholders (e.g., "Success here means a 40 percent growth rate, and a valuation of $80 million in five years, which represents an 8X return on investment for the most recent investors, and an average of $366,000 in equity value for employees.")

- The risk involved (e.g., "The existing competition, slow-moving customer base, and potential for technology disruption puts this strategy at a 60 percent likelihood of success per the plan, 20 percent likelihood of not creating value, and a 20 percent chance of losing value for investors.")

I did this exercise recently and came up with three hypotheses for the business in question: a "get profitable" low-impact strategy, a "raise a modest amount and grow thoughtfully" strategy, and a "go big" strategy. Having each of these hypotheses written down and listing their associated risks and rewards, what we needed to validate, and what we would have needed to implement for each of them made it easy to communicate the options to the board and team. Your version may have two "go big" options or only one "get profitable" and one "grow thoughtfully." It's helpful to visualize your choices.

Deciding which hypothesis to test first is complex. I want to say there's a formula, but it's typically more intuitive. Having your options on one page ensures a shared language and decision-making model. It's also an interesting test of whether there is a clear favorite among the team—a path that excites most people.

You'll spend hundreds, if not thousands, of hours testing each idea to decide which path to pursue, so take the time to choose wisely. Once you select the hypothesis to test, add it to your one-page plan and tell the team what you will set out to learn over what timeframe.

Be sure to clarify beyond a doubt that this is a process of hypothesis testing, not a decision on strategy. Otherwise, your people might interpret it as the company's direction. At one company, our sales team got involved in some experimental pitches we were making to a potential new vertical market. They became so excited they started building campaigns to market this new idea to companies. I took the blame and clarified that this was a new, untested opportunity and that we wouldn't add it to the core engine of the business until the need, value proposition, and business model were solidified.

4. TEST YOUR HYPOTHESES

It's critical to test your hypotheses thoroughly. I find interviews are vital to the process, and I like doing 100 for each hypothesis before determining the path the company should take. Not only does that mitigate risk, but it opens you up to ideas and insights.

In a transformed company, your interviewees may be half current customers and stakeholders and the other half people who don't know your company yet. So, you may have two different pitch decks for each audience, depending on how related the new direction is to your core offering.

Present interviewees with a high-level pitch on the new offering or strategy, then embrace a spirit of curiosity and ask lots of questions. You may decide to pull the plug on a hypothesis after 30 interviews. However, if you make it to 100 and are still (or more) excited about the strategy, you're likely to be on to something big, even if it's not in line with your original hypothesis.

If you can build a prototype of your offering, doing so will enhance this process dramatically. But if that is too expensive and time-consuming, do your best with slides, mockups, designs, and anything else that helps people understand the concept.

When I conduct these interviews, I like to set the stage by asking interviewees about their roles and environment and their perspective on what works and doesn't about it (e.g., "How do you feel about the accounts payable process today? What's painful about it?"). I then present our understanding of the current situation in the market and the pain points most experience in it. I like to ensure alignment between what they say and what we understand. I follow up with our proposed solution and a screenshot or image of what the offering might look like.

I take five minutes to frame the problem and solution. The rest of the time, I ask questions based on where the interviewee goes in the conversation (e.g., "You mentioned purchasing coffee for your employees is time-consuming. Would a model that uses real-time automated inventory and employee surveys like this be helpful?"). You may have "back pocket" slides at the ready based on where the conversation goes.

Ask open-ended questions that get these prospects chattering like a gossipy schoolkid, but with enough guardrails that they don't go off in useless directions. Even their tone of voice and body language can be helpful information. Be sure to engage them in stream-of-consciousness thinking, which may reveal gold nuggets of insight. Clinging too closely to your questions can stifle conversation and potentially give you insufficient data. Have two or three "must-ask" questions about your offering or strategy and leave it at that. Some questions to consider include the following:

- What did you like about this potential offering? What did you dislike? What did you need help understanding to assess its overall value?

- How would you describe this offering to your team, boss, or friend? What pain points would you say it relieves? What opportunities does it open?

- How do you alleviate these pain points today that our product could help resolve? Is it working?

- What other products would you compare it to? How do these other products fall short?

- What would make this a must-have for you? Why?

- Who on your team would love it, and who would not?

- What features would you expect?

- What would make it a dream product or service? Or what would it do if you had a magic wand to make this product do what you want? (These have always been some of the most revealing and essential questions I ask.)

- What would prevent you from trying this offering in the first place? Is there an easy way to feel comfortable trying it out before you commit?

- Would others need to be involved in the decision to buy it? If so, who?

- How much would you pay for it? (Many people like to be friendly and tell you what you want to hear. This question can be uncomfortable, but it is an excellent test to see if they genuinely lean in. Even better, ask them if they're willing to invest money to be a beta partner.)

Remember, you're not in sales mode but deep learning mode. Some of these conversations may lead to opportunities, but you'll ruin the process if you come on too strong during the research phase. And because you have a healthy core business, the interviews should be asked in the spirit of curiosity rather than with the existential dread and ticking clock typical of traditional venture-backed startup research.

Observe your interviewees: What do they most want? Are people leaning in with a checkbook and asking to have it tomorrow? Or are they merely saying nice things about your idea? When did they perk up the most? You must avoid "confirmation bias," where you seek information that validates what you already believe to be true. Choosing the right strategic move is a monumental decision, which must be backed by accurate data and, ideally, customer commitments to spending money on your new offering.

After each set of interviews, revisit your assumptions and questions. If multiple interviewees suggest that the hypothesis needs tweaking, either make the changes to the pitch or turn the potential modification into a validating question for future interviewees (e.g., "Other people have suggested a per-user pricing model would be best; describe how you would imagine paying."). Avoid making sweeping changes due to one bad interview, but instead thoughtfully refine the hypotheses as needed over time.

5. CHOOSE A STRATEGIC MOVE . . . OR WAIT

After conducting a statistically significant number of interviews, you will have enough data and stories to validate your hypotheses and decide whether to pursue that strategy, how you would follow it, and over what period.

What will likely happen is that, like the children's game of telephone, the idea has changed dramatically by the time you get through 100 interviews. And maybe several competing ideas started to weave together into something entirely different.

Deciding on a strategy is more akin to writing a great song. It may start with a random bolt of inspiration, but it takes a lot of blood, sweat, tears, experimentation, and refinement to bring the song to life. The harder you work, the more room there is for magic and luck. The "1 percent inspiration and 99 percent perspiration" adage fits well when figuring out your breakaway strategy.

Deciding on a strategy will likely be a long process. A strong core puts your company in a position where you don't have to devise a brilliant idea to survive. You can take your time and come up with the *right* idea . . . or let it come to you. If you're struggling with whether to pursue a strategy, even after many interviews, here are some questions to help determine whether you're on the right track. The strategy you are considering doesn't need to meet all these criteria (the only two must-haves are at the end of the list), but as you wrestle with a decision, the answers to these questions can shed light on whether it's the right one:

- **Connects to your core:** Does this strategy capitalize on your company's biggest strength? The closer your strategy is to your unique strength, the stronger your value proposition and the more sustainable your differentiation. Where will you source the intellectual property (IP) and talent to deliver on the strategy if it does not stem from your core?

- **Serves a large market:** How big is the addressable market? How will you segment that market? What segment is the best starting point? An ideal scenario is a massive market over the long run, but a small entry segment (beachhead) where you can prove the new strategy. (See chapter 7 on how to size your market.)

- **Centers on a critical insight:** Your strategic move should capitalize on a big, easy-to-understand idea that will cement your differentiation in customers' minds. For example, consider how Beats by Dre looked at the technical, audiophile-dominated headphone market and saw the opportunity for a motivational, strong lifestyle brand— they took positioning cues from Nike and Apple, brought it to an unsuspecting market, and built a juggernaut. (See chapter 7 on how to tell a big story to the market.)

- **Supports a significant pain point:** Did the interviews lead you to believe the pain point your strategic move will solve was a massive challenge for people? Would customers jump at your solution? Did they want to pay you money or be an early customer? Meeting this criterion is essential but can sometimes be challenging to determine early on, especially for more innovative solutions (e.g., no one knew they wanted an iPhone until they saw it). Ensure that your potential customers are leaning in heavily.

- **Provides an unfair advantage:** Is this a difficult-to-copy strategic move that could de-position competitors? Does this strategy provide you with network effects or a competitive moat? Sometimes, startups confuse a cool new feature with a strategy. When you play out your strategic move over the long run, you want to have developed enough protection to maintain that differentiation over the long run, either through brand identity, network effects, market dominance, or economies of scale.

- **Capitalizes on a trend:** Can you point to a significant technology or social trend that supports this strategy? Can you beat your competition in the way you embrace that trend? Meeting this practical criterion ensures you are ahead of the technology curve and serves as a positioning element that will help tell your story. A breakaway move is contingent on being the innovative player who understands where the world is headed and can deliver on that future.

- **Excites your team (must-have):** Do your execs, board members, and employees love this strategy? Would they be thrilled to be a part of it? Pursuing a breakaway strategy requires discipline, focus, creativity, and effort. You may have a few detractors, but at least 80 percent of stakeholders should be leaning in. You need every ounce of energy from your team. It's vital to ensure they feel a part of the process and are proud of the idea and its execution.

- **Is feasible (must-have):** Can you execute this strategy with your current resources? Does your team believe it's doable? This is an easy concept to understand but a challenging one to validate. If you are burning cash and only have six months left of runway, is it feasible to launch a new product?

These criteria are guideposts for validating your potential strategy, but not hard and fast rules. There will always be room for intuition, conviction, and a "screw it, let's do it" (to quote

Sir Richard Branson) decision. But it's key to consider where you could get stuck or blindsided before letting excitement and momentum drive the decision.

Can you choose more than one move to make? Not really. Your move may have many elements to ensure its success (you could say "sub-moves") and a timeline of what needs to happen and when. But a company should only have one breakaway move at a time. Choose it wisely.

SAMI INKINEN:
HOW TO ORCHESTRATE A BREAKOUT

Sami Inkinen will make even the best of us feel like lazy schlubs. He's the co-founder and CEO of Virta Health, which provides the first clinically proven treatment program to reverse type 2 diabetes without medications or surgery. He is also a venture partner at Obvious Ventures. He was also co-founder and COO of the massive real estate marketplace Trulia, which went public in 2012 and then merged with Zillow in 2015. Sami is also a world-class athlete, having won his age group in the Ironman race and completing the race seven times. He even rowed from California to Hawaii with his wife, unsupported, to raise awareness of sugar's connection to diabetes. He has an excellent mind for strategy and the experience to back it up.

What's the key to finding a breakout move?
You must be in the right market at the right time. VCs always debate the age-old question of whether the founder or market is most important. I believe the market always wins, and you can't

continued

control its timing. The big challenge is finding founder-market fit: identifying a large, underserved market and ensuring you are the right team to execute it. If you have that in place, you must build a contrarian hypothesis. You may be crazy; have a profound, unique insight; or maybe a little bit of both—but you must stand out.

What has been your biggest lesson around breakout strategies?

One of my primary VC investors at Trulia, who was also an important mentor to me, told me, "Every 18 months, you must bet the company on something." I was initially reluctant to risk my entire company on a "shoot the moon" strategy every few years. But over time, I realized he was right. To become—and remain—a category leader, you must continue to innovate on new technology.

Why do you think that's the case?

New platforms tend to come in these 18–24-month cycles, which means cheaper opportunities to innovate, like being first to a new ad platform. You need to be in front of that shift and then focus, focus, focus. It's like using a magnifying glass to start a fire: focus all the energy on one spot. If any one thing is working, do it 100X more instead of applying a peanut butter strategy. When you focus, you get disproportionate results. You don't want to be like WeWork, branching out into schools and then having to close that business later.

How did you apply that strategy at Trulia?

We started Trulia in 2004. The world had moved from portals (like Yahoo) to search (primarily Google), so we built the first real estate listing service based on search. We eventually figured out the breakaway channel, SEO [search engine optimization], which made the company. We focused all our energy on SEO and became the best in the world at delivering real estate listings through search. If you took that away, the value of the company was gone. We had to bet the company again when the iPhone came out. SEO was no longer as relevant in a mobile-first world, and 18 months after its introduction, half of our business came through mobile. We almost missed that trend but thankfully got our app out in time. You must be paranoid about platform shifts and pay close attention to these changes.

How do you figure out the right market and business model?
I start with a big problem that isn't going away anytime soon. At Trulia, it was recognizing that there was a consumer internet destination for every classified category except real estate. At Virta, it is diabetes, which is a huge problem that is massively detrimental clinically and economically. Figuring out how to commercialize a big idea like this takes a long process of experimentation. No amount of McKinsey analysis will get you that answer. Instead, you have to have a beginner's mind and learn by doing: Be humble and listen, listen, listen. Also, don't try to innovate on multiple axes at one time. Building a new product and service is innovating on one axis; trying to be too clever by innovating on a new business model simultaneously will often confuse your buyer and slow growth.

What if You Can't Find a Breakaway Move?

The process I described for finding a breakaway move has served me well as an entrepreneur. But it's no guarantee that following it will help uncover the perfect strategy to dominate your market. Maybe there is no breakaway move to be found.

Or perhaps it's not the right time, or you aren't resourced to execute it. That's okay. If you haven't landed on a breakaway move, here are your options:

- **Keep trying**: Seek out your breakaway move over a more extended period. Keep the process going in the background, but don't push too hard for a decision if it's not the right move or you're not ready. It can take years. Every time you investigate a new idea, seeds will be planted, even if you don't choose to pursue those strategies. Find solace in the fact that you're building an extensive database of feedback, ideas, and market knowledge that will make finding that breakaway move easier when the time is right.

- **Take a break**: Focus on moderate growth areas and smaller markets where you have a strong advantage. Take time from the process outlined in this chapter and focus on your core business. Keep a notebook of possible insights that could drive your strategy in the future, and only pursue them when you feel ready or when there is a significant demand from the market. You can always keep your eyes open for a more substantial opportunity and potential moves.

- **Focus on profits**: Operate the business profitably with less focus on growth. Sometimes, there isn't a breakaway move to make. That's okay. It's better to admit that fact than to try and force a strategy you won't be able to deliver on. Building the value in your company will likely need to be based more on cash flows and modest growth. This strategy is the equivalent of your "safety school" when you applied to college—it may not be your first choice, but it is good and can still create significant value for shareholders.

That's precisely what happened at Monsoon, the company I discussed at the end of the previous chapter. Once we stabilized the business, we tested growth opportunities. We conducted experiments and built prototypes. Ultimately, the CEO and I concluded that we didn't have the product, market, or internal DNA to execute a breakaway move. This business could earn 30 percent profits, which can be exceedingly valuable. It would be better to distribute the profits, invest them into other businesses, or sell the company. Instead of forcing growth, we turned Monsoon into a stable, profitable business that kept its customers happy and productive.

A breakaway move can't be forced. As a leader, you do your best to find it, but it may take years or not be in the company's DNA. The team's skills, experience, and ambitions are most important in finding and executing a breakaway strategy, but timing, circumstance, and luck play a role too.

Hard Lessons

Many years ago, I was approached by a $70 million customer service outsourcing company to evaluate if there was a breakaway move for them to pursue. The company's core business offered at-home agents to augment internal customer service departments during peak periods, such as the holidays, when those companies didn't have enough employees to support the demand.

Growth had stalled after numerous CEOs, failed strategies, and the loss of key team members. The company was stuck. Cash was tight, and even if they could free up more, it wasn't clear where that cash should be invested. In short, they were keeping the wheels on the car but had no destination and little gas to get there. "Should we just give up and sell the company?" their board asked me, "Or is there something we can do to get growth going again?"

To figure out if there was a game-changing play they could run, I walked them through the process outlined earlier. We talked to their teams, collected information, and conducted customer interviews. We learned that their customers cared most about the quality of the agents, as opposed to pricing or systems integration of their service, and were frustrated with high turnover and apathetic agents across the industry.

The most promising hypotheses we tested suggested that, instead of competing on price while striving for a baseline service level like other companies, they should look at ways to transform the satisfaction levels of call center interactions between customers and agents. We realized the best strategic move was to address the main pain point: identify, hire, and maintain the happiest, most motivated agents.

When do contractors show that level of motivation? *When their livelihood depends on it.* Instead of relying on 9-to-5 employees in one location, the idea was to hire only friendly, independent, experienced contractors for whom this work supports their ideal life. These hires were more entrepreneurial, given the risks they took with their work. So they tried harder than the 9-to-5 employees. This strategic move capitalized on the company's history of employing work-at-home contractors but changed the practice from a structural decision into a transformative pillar of differentiation by finding and keeping the top 5 to 10 percent of contractors aligned with the new values.

The processes, metrics, technology, hiring, and ultimately, the business's new positioning had to be built around happy, motivated entrepreneurs instead of bored 9-to-5'ers. This strategy, we believed, would crush satisfaction levels and help the company avoid the race-to-the-bottom pricing game. And competitors couldn't replicate it without changing their entire operation. The board loved the strategy and decided to make a move. They brought in new cash and new executives to run the play.

But while we had ensured that our strategic move covered most of the bases listed earlier, it failed to meet two very critical ones. First, the move did not excite the old-guard employees who were stuck in their ways and had too much PTSD from previous leadership regimes and failed initiatives. This move threatened some employees' jobs and inadvertently created an old versus new regime conflict, which might bring down the company if not handled well.

Secondly, it was not feasible with the current resources—it required a more innovative team, lots of systems rebuilding, and a bold marketing and positioning process, which the board and leadership were not ready to take on. As solid as a breakaway strategy as it may have appeared to be at face value, it wasn't the right strategic growth path for the organization. They couldn't deliver on it.

The early transformation phase is about focus, not unbridled ambition. This is why it's essential to streamline the business first—to make it as effective and profitable as possible around its core business—before experimenting with growth. When the company is healthy, it's the ideal environment to patiently test for growth opportunities. That can be hard for founders or new leaders trained to hit the gas quickly. You need the time and space to find your growth path—that's the essence of the breakaway turnaround.

CHAPTER 6

Scale Intelligently — Maximize Scale, Minimize Dilution

Let your performance do the thinking.

—CHARLOTTE BRONTË

Guru Hariharan, a former hotshot from Amazon's data science team, was the founding CEO of Boomerang Commerce, a software business that helped retailers price their products by comparing them to competitors. Soon after he started Boomerang in 2012, the startup grew nicely, signing contracts with large retailers like Home Depot, Staples, and Best Buy, which relied on Boomerang's data engine to optimize sales and profits. But things had gone sideways by 2016 when I came on as a coach and then a board member.

Financially, the company looked strong, with over $12 million in sales and a decent balance sheet. But Amazon's online dominance was killing retailers who could no longer compete, ushering in the "Retail Apocalypse" that would eventually take down big retailers like Borders, Toys "R" Us, and Sears. It was hard to sell the same products as Amazon for less money without the "one-click shop" ease. Boomerang was serving a dying market. Guru knew it would die alongside their customers if the company didn't transform.

But Guru had already raised two funding rounds and couldn't raise more, given the market conditions. He needed to act. But how?

Since Boomerang was a vertical software business, they had developed excellent relationships with C-level executives in retail organizations. These experts helped the team understand the shift from brick-and-mortar to digital marketplaces like Amazon, Walmart, and Instacart. It became clear to Guru that brands, not retailers, would succeed in the Amazon era. Strong brands with unique products and good stories that capture consumer loyalty would continue to thrive regardless of the retail channel. So, for Boomerang, it would be better to serve a consumer-packaged goods company like Hershey—with deep customer loyalty—rather than the stores selling Hershey products. And since these brands were new to e-commerce, which would ultimately become a significant channel for sales, they needed help orchestrating that process.

To survive, Boomerang would have to shift its focus from retailers to large brands. But it would need to build a new product for this market—a massive undertaking. It's one thing to help companies sell commodity products where the data is clear (e.g., all retailers sell the same Nikon camera with the same attributes). But how could Boomerang translate its core strength—turning e-commerce data into intelligent actions—to serve brands with unique products? And how could it orchestrate such an ambitious pivot while running out of money?

Guru's first move was to raise a debt line against their ARR. This gave the company some cushion to start the transformation without raising equity financing, which would have severely diluted the existing investors. This immediate financial relief gave the team conviction that they would have the time and resources to build an initial minimum viable product (MVP) for this new market.

As they got deeper into the product and market requirements, they came to a significant decision: they would sell the old retail business to finance the new brand business. While Boomerang's R&D team cranked on the new product, Guru hired bankers and prepared the retail business for sale. Initially, Guru was stymied by the process. No one wanted a company that targeted dying retailers. But Boomerang had done such a good job building a "mission-critical" application for its customers that those customers became potential buyers. Eventually, the home improvement chain Lowe's leaned in with the best offer. Lowe's could use the technology and team to improve pricing and merchandising capabilities, which could become a competitive advantage.

The sale of its retail business gave Boomerang at least a three-year runway of non-dilutive capital. With a complete focus on its core strength and new business—and with healthy cash in the bank—the company was reborn as CommerceIQ, dedicated to helping brands optimize their market share on e-commerce marketplaces.

What happened next was staggering. The team, now smaller, leaner, focused, and more regimented, delivered the product to market on time, on budget, and with a value proposition that hit a huge pain point with buyers. Large brands didn't take long to learn about this "new kid on the block" who had made a big splash in retail and was now a transformed company, helping its customers modernize their multi-channel approach.

Within a few years, CommerceIQ had surpassed the old business in revenue. Thanks to Guru and the team's execution and vision—and a healthy balance sheet—the company became the market leader in their new category: e-commerce channel optimization (ECO). Three years after selling the retail business, CommerceIQ raised a $125 million round of growth capital at a valuation of over $1 billion, and the company is still going strong as of this writing.

I have not witnessed many transformations as well executed as CommerceIQ's. And thankfully, I got a front-row seat. It is a case study of making a "bet the company" move when market conditions are whittling away your options.

The Smart Growth Path for You

If, like Guru, you shot for the stars and missed the first time around, you will naturally be more grounded in market, product, and execution realities on your second try. Like a broken vase glued back together, the healed cracks might still show, but your company is stronger than before.

Based on a clear understanding of market realities, the conviction of your team, and the work from the last chapter, your growth path will likely fall into one of these three categories:

1. **Stay the course:** If a breakaway move is unclear, staying within your current market and seeking conservative growth or maximizing profitability is ideal. A breakaway move may reveal itself over time but can't be forced.

2. **Expand cautiously:** If you uncovered a market strategy that supports healthy—but not breakout—growth rates (likely somewhere between 20 to 50 percent), you can build a plan to capitalize on this opportunity profitably or with modest funding. (I discuss options to source that funding later in this chapter.)

3. **Scale quickly:** Congrats! You found a breakaway move that capitalizes on your core strength and takes you into a larger, winnable market. This path will likely require more significant funding, but you have options. And the amount of funding you raise and whom you raise it from will be based on sales and marketing data, not wishful thinking.

Regardless of the path, the complex set of variables you've identified while working through the previous chapters and your hard-earned wisdom from going through the transformation will illuminate the way. Approaching the process with a healthy, thoughtful mix of vision and pragmatism—think Steve Jobs meets Warren Buffett—is your best bet. In this chapter, I'll show you how to build a Growth Plan that supports this kind of intelligent scaling.

JODI SHERMAN JAHIC: FREEDOM IS NOT NEEDING MORE MONEY

Jodi Sherman Jahic is not your typical venture capitalist. While most VCs assume one out of 10 portfolio companies will be a big winner that makes the fund its money, Jodi seeks successful outcomes for all her companies through capital efficiency and a deep, unwavering focus on customers. She is the co-founder of Aligned Partners—a firm named for the desire to align the investors' interests with those of the founders. Before Aligned, she was a partner at Voyager Capital; a co-founder and managing director of SCG, a pledge fund focused on capital-efficient investments; a Kauffman Fellow at Battery Ventures; and a co-founder of three startups.

What do most founders get wrong about funding?

That funding should come before you discover product/market fit. There are a lot of founders who start their process by seeking seed funding and who see raising money as evidence of success. But the only real evidence of success is customers who can quantitatively say why they're happy. In one of his shareholder letters, Jeff Bezos wrote that there are many axes to differentiate your company (price, technology, product). But the only way to grow in the long run is to be customer-focused. That should be the founders' guiding light, not how much they can raise.

Where does that pressure to raise money come from?

First, it comes from the overstated belief that if a competitor raises money, you will be disadvantaged if you don't raise a similar amount. Getting the value proposition right is much more important—you are a foundationless house without it. Second, the pressure to raise money comes from the financial industry: As funds have increased, the rounds have also. The supply of companies hasn't increased in line with the investment demand. Third, the pressure is social: Raising money is high status and validating, and there's a lot you can do with the money. But raising too much is where most companies get in trouble.

Where did your philosophy of company building come from?

My father was an entrepreneur who started six companies, all still running, and only one took outside investment. He taught me that the only freedom is not needing more money. Founding a company consumes your life for 10 years: It can break up marriages and hurt relationships with children. And yet three-quarters of founders never see a dime from their startup. It kills me to see poor fundraising strategies that limit the reward for founders. I want to be the last money the company ever raises and help its leaders build their company in a smarter way where everyone can win.

What gives founders their best chance at seeing a reward for their work?

Focus. The discipline of saying no. All the details are in your GTM strategy: How do you reduce the variables? Like crossing the chasm, the less you do at the beginning, the better. Solve one problem quantitatively and qualitatively better than any competitor. Facebook started with Harvard and honed the site before expanding users to other schools and beyond. Amazon started selling only books and went public after raising only $9

continued

million. There's a temptation to solve more problems when you raise more money. You need to turn down almost everything to achieve greatness.

How do you know it's the right time to "add gas" and grow faster?

When you are sure that gas will create more fire. It's about repeatable processes: You need evidence that your strategy will work. If you have two salespeople and it's working, you can't go straight to hiring 10, but maybe you could go from two to six. You operate from a spirit of pursuing the truth, not the desire to build a graph that goes up and down to the right. Sometimes, the best role I can play for my CEOs is seeking disconfirming evidence because founders can be wrapped inside the story. As physicist Richard Feynman said, "The first principle is that you must not fool yourself—and you are the easiest person to fool."

How to Build a Growth Plan

If you decide to expand cautiously or if you've found your breakaway strategy and want to scale quickly, you will need a roadmap to get there. Some people call this roadmap a "strategic plan" or a "business plan." I find that the term "strategic plan," on the one hand, is open to broad interpretation and generally focused on "how" your company will win. As a result, many strategic plans are too high-level and aspirational. On the other hand, the outdated term "business plan" instantly recalls the opposite: a bloated, overly detailed document that doesn't allow much maneuverability.

What I call a "Growth Plan" is the practical middle ground

between broad strategic plans and inflexible business plans. It seeks to answer the question, "What resources do we need over what period to deliver on our growth strategy?" It is revised frequently, as its objective is to plan for smart growth based on the pull of the market. This plan validates your assumptions, communicates strategy to the team, and ensures you find the proper funding for your business if needed.

What I cover in this chapter may seem old hat to some people, especially those with a finance background. However, I am going deep on it for several reasons: (1) many founders have never had to go this deep on their Growth Planning and may not have the skill set; (2) if the company was venture-backed, chances are the operating plan was less critical as the situation changed so frequently; and (3) the types of investors you may need to woo for this phase of transformation will be much more focused on the operating plan, both to justify the investment as well as track progress toward the shared goals. That said, if you have the skills to articulate a three- to five-year Growth Plan and use it to raise funding from the right type of investor, you can skim this chapter or skip to chapter 7.

To create a Growth Plan, you first need to clarify your market. This will include your initial buyer focus—your "ideal customer profile (ICP)" or your beachhead market—and the follow-on markets you will likely pursue after testing and validation. Second, translate these decisions into a three-year forecast to anticipate how you will achieve those market goals. Finally, you must zero in on the best metrics to measure the progress against your Growth Plan.

Your marketing leader(s) should be heavily involved in this process, as the results will dictate their priorities for the coming years. As you create your Growth Plan, document it so you can go back to it regularly and update it as necessary.

1. DEFINE YOUR MARKETS

The foundation of our Growth Plan is a clear understanding of your initial market focus and the follow-on markets you will likely pursue after testing and validation. To get started, articulate, in detail, your assumptions about your target customers and determine when you will go after each customer segment. This exercise is not about detailing how you will win those markets (differentiators, positioning, etc.), which should have been done as part of the breakaway strategy work in the previous chapter. At this point, we are focused on how your chosen markets will support the growth you need.

When analyzing current or target markets, startups often see buyer segments as one big morass of potential customers (i.e., "If we capture just 5 percent of this $10 billion market . . ."). Leaders often don't dig into the nuances of their markets, creating downstream confusion and leading to mixed-up priorities. For example, a company may see 501(c)(3) charity organizations as its market but not look at funding sources, the size of their addressable audience, or what geography they serve, all of which would change their buying patterns. A true understanding of a market often comes too late. If you're going through a transformation, you likely have a deeply analyzed, experience-driven understanding of your market and how to navigate its labyrinth of buyer types and patterns.

The most common approach to doing a top-down analysis of your current and future markets is to measure your total available market (TAM), serviceable addressable market (SAM), and serviceable obtainable market (SOM):

TAM: The total number of possible customers in the market multiplied by the average price of your product or service for each segment. If you sell services to domestic car dealerships, for example, you could use a data analytics company like Dun & Bradstreet (D&B), census data, or a list builder to come up with the number of all dealerships of a specific size in the United States and multiply it by your average deal size (possibly segmented by size such that smaller dealerships would pay $5,000/year while larger ones would pay $15,000/year). Sometimes research firms like Forrester or Gartner define the size of markets, which can be helpful as a data point but hard to defend as the basis for strategy. The nuance of their analysis may not map cleanly to your strategy. The more targeted your market is, the more valuable a TAM analysis is because it helps you with your long- and short-term strategies.

TAM is typically used for long-term planning, raising capital, understanding exit multiples, and providing the context for your SAM (see following text). Investors see TAM as a shorthand snapshot of how big your company could be and to gauge the range of its exit options. When calculating your TAM, consider how your company could expand over time. For example, instead of only measuring the total available market in the United States, consider whether your company could be capable of expanding internationally in the long run.

If you're still in the early stages of your company, your TAM may be less meaningful since your product and market strategy may be in flux. Your TAM becomes more critical as the company matures and the path becomes clear. It's a great starting point for defining your market, but you need to dig deeper into the details of buyers for your analysis to impact your execution planning.

SAM: The portion of the TAM that you can *actively* go after—your targets. In the car dealership example, the SAM might represent West Coast dealerships that use a specific accounting system with which your product integrates tightly. You won't win all these potential buyers, but your offering fits their needs, and your marketing team will target them. Investors will scrutinize the SAM (whether they call it that or not) as it's the most helpful metric for understanding the likely return on their investment.

SAM is critical to your marketing efforts. I recently targeted trade associations for Mobilize. Of the roughly 100,000 trade associations in the United States, only about 8,000 had budgets large enough to afford the type of software we were selling. Within that TAM, we filtered for the type of association, ideal budget size, and whether they were innovative (because their financials are public, we could use "technology spend as a percentage of their budget" as a proxy for innovation). That left us with around 2,000 trade associations that we could actively target. Since our average deal size for those buyers was $30,000 per year, we had a $60 million SAM compared to a much larger TAM that reflected all associations and other buyer types.

SOM: It represents the portion of the market you can realistically capture in the next two to five years. Instead of starting from the most significant market possible and getting more granular, SOM is calculated by looking at what's reasonable given your resources—number of salespeople, regional coverage, manufacturing capacity, etc.—alongside a thoughtful analysis of your historical data. Often, this historical data is overlooked by leaders who prefer to look forward, especially in a turnaround situation where things are constantly changing. But unless you have entirely pivoted to new products and buyers, looking at past sales productivity is one of the best ways to derive a realistic SOM. Your ability to hit your SOM goals indicates to investors that you have a good shot at your SAM—and that your company can scale efficiently.

After analyzing the TAM, SAM, and SOM, I recommend reviewing your ICP. This is your perfect, hypothetical customer, which may be segmented by size, budget, geography, related purchases, pain points, or other relevant attributes that would make a customer a great fit. If you're a consumer company, your ICP is likely the same as your buyer persona or "avatar," which includes things like age, location, income, and profession. Typically, the ICP is developed to support marketing efforts (i.e., targeting the right profiles), but I also find it good practice to develop your Growth Plan so it closely aligns with the TAM, SAM, and SOM analyses.

This market analysis will give you a strong understanding of who truly needs what you offer and how much you can grow over the long run. It's a critical exercise in solidifying your plan and finding the right investors to support it.

2. BUILD A FORECAST

Once you have clarity around your current market and the markets you plan to pursue for growth, you need to figure out how much it will cost to do it well. Will you launch a new product? Hire execs from a competitor? Merge with an adjacent player? Build strategic partnerships? Budgeting for these moves may be straightforward (e.g., "hire three new executives, expand the GTM team by 100 percent over two years, buy XYZ Corp. for $15 million in cash and equity") or more general (e.g., "merge with a company serving the adjacent category of ski apparel"). In either case, you need a conservative budget that shows what that proposed path looks like.

You likely have a budget (P&L, cash flow forecast, and balance sheet) already, though if you're like me, it may have gotten unwieldy over time and need a refresh. If so, I would encourage you to start from scratch to ensure tight alignment between the budget and your new strategy.

Most importantly, this budget keeps the board on track with the plan and ensures you close the right financing. It's also essential for your executive team to understand and commit to the plan. If you have an open work culture, the whole company may see this forecast. So, spend the time to ensure its accuracy and depth. Everyone's role and ability to make money on this venture is tied to this plan.

3. MEASURE YOUR PROGRESS

With a clear sense of your current market(s), the markets you'll pursue for later growth, the moves and resources needed, and a realistic forecast, you can zero in on the best metrics to measure progress. The metrics most helpful to get this done might differ for each company and even vary from industry to industry. In general, you want your metrics to answer the following questions:

- **How effectively do we obtain (and retain) customers?** Knowing how profitably you can grow your core business is essential. Can you acquire customers productively and count on them being with you long-term? Metrics that help you answer this question can make budgeting, decision-making, hiring, and fundraising much easier. Some commonly used metrics that would be useful include CAC, win rate, or LTV; e-commerce companies might track RoAS and conversion rates; and gaming companies might measure average revenue per user.

- **How do we finance our growth?** When you know your customer metrics, you can figure out the ideal flows of cash to support that engine. How will you reinvest profits? Will you need more money later? If so, what metrics will you need to show to raise that capital? Traditional metrics include revenue, cash, profits, and burn rate.

- **How strong and innovative is our product?** While the market is the best gauge for your product's value and differentiation, measuring how your product organization is doing against the Growth Plan is worthwhile. You can track product shipping (e.g., are you shipping on time and on budget?) and product value and differentiation (e.g., win rate, customer success rate, and customer satisfaction).

- **How is our team doing?** Measuring your employee's engagement with and commitment to your new growth strategy is difficult, but it speaks highly of management teams that prioritize it. In addition to traditional employee engagement metrics like sentiment and satisfaction, the scores that matter when it comes to the Growth Plan are around alignment with (and conviction in) the company's vision and how stretched they feel in delivering on that plan.

Dashboards provide a clear visualization of a company's progress against its plan. The best dashboards are easy to understand, meaningful, and tell a compelling story about the financial and strategic health of the company. In my experience, however, they are challenging to create. They often pull the wrong data or misrepresent the story behind the data, which causes confusion, arguments, and poor decision-making. If you create a dashboard, keep it simple but accurate. Instead of aiming for perfection, focus on the metrics that can't be obfuscated or misinterpreted. Fewer valid metrics are better than copious suspect metrics.

As a transformation leader, the metrics you share with investors, board, and team should have the simplicity and elegance of an Apple product and the clarity of the atomic clock. Why? Because businesses succeed or fail based on communication of data. Poorly collected data, misinterpreted meanings, and overly rosy outlooks are the biggest reasons companies get stuck. Getting the correct numbers may require hard work, but it's worth it. A good dashboard is a clear and compelling testament to the ideal growth path.

Financing Your Growth Plan

Once you have a well-researched, agreed-upon Growth Plan, you'll need to decide how to fund it. With the rise of new technologies, plug-and-play infrastructure, and a booming tech market, we've witnessed not only the explosion of startups, but of new ways to finance them. Navigating all the funding options can be tricky.

Here is a breakdown of some of the most common and appropriate financing strategies based on your growth path: Stay the course, expand cautiously, or grow quickly. These funding strategies don't always fit neatly into each path, so you should always consider all options, including those not listed here.

IF YOU CHOOSE TO STAY THE COURSE

If you decide to remain on your current trajectory and are not already profitable but can be with some additional financing, consider the following avenues for funding your Growth Plan goals:

- **Bootstrapping:** Growing organically is an excellent path if you can manage it. If the market isn't pulling you into faster growth, don't force it. A larger market may reveal itself over time, but if you're profitable, you'll have time to allow that. In the meantime, investors won't be breathing down your neck for unrealistic growth. Ensure everyone on the cap table (the list of people and firms who own the business) is aligned and supportive.

- **Loan or line of credit:** If you have enough revenue and predictability in your business, you can structure a loan from your bank or a loan specialist. Just be aware of the covenants that come with that debt. I've been involved with many businesses painted into a corner by covenants they couldn't live up to. For example, the lender asks you to maintain 30 percent growth rates, but to get that growth requires spending on sales and marketing that drains the cash you do have. Note that banks usually have more favorable interest rates than specialty firms but may not be as flexible with loan terms, and you usually must use them as your primary bank.

- **"Friends and family":** Like bootstrapping, financing through your network or the company's can quickly and flexibly bridge the gap to the company's next stage. You can structure it as debt or equity and keep the terms simple and aligned with your desired outcomes.

- **Customer financing:** Another path to organic growth is having customers fund the development of new products. Like a Kickstarter for B2B companies, this model allows companies to target customers with pain points they can solve and charge them for early access to the product, features they need, and a chance to influence its direction. Jive was funded this way. Sun Microsystems desperately wanted Jive's product (which at the time was open source) but had a list of features they needed before using it. Jive's contract with Sun Microsystems paid for the new product development that started the business.

IF YOU CHOOSE TO EXPAND CAUTIOUSLY

If the company has a modest but respectable growth outlook (for now), consider the following options to exploit the opportunity without sacrificing the likelihood of success:

- **Venture debt:** A less dilutive and more flexible alternative to traditional fundraising, venture debt is a loan backed up with warrants to purchase equity later if the investor chooses (e.g., rights to buy shares equal to 5 percent of the total loan amount). This debt comes with covenants and reporting requirements like the above-mentioned bank loans.

- **Bridge financing:** This interim loan or equity investment "bridges" a company to the next significant financing event (e.g., the next round of funding, reaching profitability, or getting acquired). For traditional startups, bridge financing often takes the form of a convertible note that converts at a discount in future funding rounds or a liquidity event or allows warrants to purchase equity. It's a good option if you have a clear milestone and a path to get there.

- **Angels:** If you don't need a large round of funding, individual investors could be a good option for retaining autonomy while having a flexible investment structure. Individual investors don't have limited partners to report back to like VC or PE firms (the institutions that invest in their funds) do, so you can set the terms that work for you (e.g., whether it is debt or equity or how it fits into the cap table).

- **Family offices:** Unlike private equity and VC firms, family offices invest the money from a single wealthy family. This means they can be flexible with their terms and investment strategies since they don't have to report back to limited partners. So, they can operate like angel investors but with the ability to write larger checks. If your Growth Plan doesn't fit the growth profile that VC and PE firms expect (including risk, cash flow, time to liquidity, market size, or other strategic characteristics) but still represents a potentially significant return on investment, funding from a family office could be a good option.

- **Private equity:** Since PE firms typically buy a majority (or significant minority stake) of the companies, getting funding from them is a weightier decision than getting funding through the other options in this list. PE may be your best bet if you have a clear path to growth and profitability that would make your company worth three to five times what it's worth today.

You may need to clean up the cap table before PE funding is an option, as many firms don't get involved if there are many other investors because the controls, decision-making, and investor rights are muddled. Beyond providing growth capital, they can also offer operational and strategic support, assist with acquiring other companies, improve corporate governance, and possibly buy some of your shares so that you feel more comfortable with the risks in the next growth phase. As discussed in chapter 1, find a firm that shares your vision, can add value through practical assistance, and with whom you have a strong connection.

IF YOU CHOOSE TO SCALE QUICKLY

If the company is clearly on a strong growth trajectory—40 to 100 percent annual growth for a $5 million to $20 million revenue business—consider these financing options to support that growth:

- **Private equity**: As described earlier, PE is a good option when the growth outlook is clear. Because PE firms vary in their risk profiles, there may be a firm that aligns with your more ambitious Growth Plan.

- **Venture capital:** Consider a VC round if you want a healthy infusion of cash with less equity dilution than you'd likely get with a PE investment. However, you are setting a high bar for your company's performance, and like with PE, you are agreeing to liquidity within a specific timeframe, so make sure you believe in the Growth Plan agreed to when you raise. Remember that most VCs make their money from only 10 percent of their companies becoming massive, so you need to have a deep conviction in your ability to execute.

- **Asset sale:** If, like Boomerang, your company has become a "two-headed monster" with two increasingly separate lines of business, a good option might be to sell off one line of business and use the cash to support the rapid growth of the other business. The downside of this approach is that selling a business line can take a lot of time and energy and distract you from running the other business. And you may ultimately not get the value you imagined for the asset you are selling. Before going in this direction, talk to bankers and insiders about comparable transactions ("comps") to understand the opportunity.

- **Strategic investors:** Sometimes called corporate venture capital (CVC), strategic investors are the investment groups inside large corporations that invest directly into companies or alongside traditional venture firms. The downside of working with strategic investors is that partnering with one company can hinder your relationships with their competitors. Make sure you're not sabotaging later growth by getting into bed with one company.

This is not a complete list of financing options. New hybrid funding sources are popping up constantly. So, take time to find the best fit for the path you've decided to take. But regardless of how you fund your Growth Plan, *raise only what you need to execute the plan with a bit of cushion.* Sure, funding from VC and PE firms might come with perks, such as operating teams that should be factored in. But that assistance should be baked into the Growth Plan's assumptions. Remember: Less-experienced founders brag about how much they raised; more experienced founders brag about how little. Only raise when it's irresponsible *not* to.

On the Right Path

With a solid Growth Plan and appropriate financing securely in place, the stage is set to build your second-act startup. At this point, you know what mountain you are climbing and have the resources to get there. You have a strong core and early indications of expansion from that core. You're on the right path.

Making it this far is a massive feat. You've gotten through the most challenging part: you reconciled with your past challenges, stripped the business down to its essence, and earned the right to keep the company alive. You've proven that you're capable of difficult decisions and profound change. And now you are on track with a more thoughtful, deliberate, and focused company. Emerging from the dark forest of transformation, it's time to be reborn to the market. The old company has died a ritualistic death, and the new company is emerging after its metamorphosis. It's time to let the world know what you're about. It's time to tell your story.

Hard Lessons

In 2018, I acquired a community software company called Mobilize. The Israeli-founded startup had raised $8 million in funding but never really got off the ground. It had a good product but negligible revenue when I acquired it. Having spent time in the category with Jive, I believed I could find a market and get it going.

I got the company lean, focused on its core (membership organizations like trade associations), and built a new GTM strategy around this segment. The problem was that the target segment moved slowly, and an entrenched vendor who had been in the space for a while was "good enough." Since revenue was starting from almost nothing, I couldn't achieve the needed growth rates to make it profitable, so I kept having to put more money in.

After several years, we had a good team and a newly rebuilt product, but the infrastructure was costly. Instead of selling the business, I merged it with a profitable one, Monsoon, the book-selling software company you may recall from chapter 4.

The thinking was that the profits from Monsoon would bridge the gap to Mobilize's profitability. I also brought in a CEO to run the Growth Plan and, if it didn't work, to orchestrate the sale of Mobilize.

Things seemed okay at first as the CEO got to know the business. However, the newer sales team didn't know the membership organization market well enough and couldn't hit the conservative numbers we set. In addition to the market challenges, the operating plan built by our team and accountants had missed critical cash flow assumptions. The budget was flawed, and the cash from Monsoon couldn't cover the Mobilize losses. We were forced to take on debt capital to cover the shortfall.

We brought in an experienced part-time CFO to develop a more realistic operating plan, which clarified that we couldn't keep operating the business with the current team and modest growth rate. The market headwinds were too strong. We didn't have enough money, and I didn't see the point of taking on more financing for the company's value potential.

The options at that point were to streamline the team even more than we had (including offshoring the engineering) or to sell the business to a buyer who needed the product and the team. I really liked the employees and wanted them to stay together, so opted for the latter. We found a company that was a perfect fit, and the sale went through swimmingly.

The lesson? Don't trust the Growth Plan unless it's simple and straightforward, and you have your fingerprints all over it. And if your business is complicated at all, have an expert review it thoroughly. It's worth the expense to have peace of mind and conviction in your ability to execute.

CHAPTER 7

Tell Your New Story— Position Yourself, De-position Others

Why fit in when you were born to stand out?

—DR. SEUSS

Nate Quigley was pulling his hair out.

It was 2013. He was two and a half years into his photo-sharing company, Chatbooks, and he was stuck. Although he was an experienced founder with two successful companies behind him, he couldn't get this one off the ground. Adding to his stress was that this was personal: He believed passionately in Chatbooks' profound purpose to help families safeguard, organize, and enjoy their memories.

But customers weren't coming. Their photo collection application had all the features customers said they wanted. But getting them to use the product was like pulling teeth. After digging into why, the beta customers responded: "It's too complicated." Very few households had the time and tech skills across the family to learn and use the software. Nate was demoralized. He was ready to pull the plug.

One evening, while Nate was in his home office, his wife, Vanessa, was in their five-year-old son Declan's bedroom a few doors down, getting him ready for bed. Declan was having an emotional moment. "I wish I didn't have to grow older," he told her, clutching an older picture of the family and wishing he could return to that time.

After looking at printed photos of the family and having a poignant conversation about the passage of time, Vanessa finally put him down to sleep. Then, she joined Nate in his office. She sat in a chair and, in a moment that would become a profound part of the company's creation myth, said, "I wish you could just print my Instagram."

Vanessa had been curating family photos on the popular photo-sharing social media platform to preserve memories and share them with her family. She wanted to give those images to her son. But Declan wasn't hugging the smartphone. He was grasping the printed images of the family. The photos were a totem—a powerful, physical connection to their past.

In one epiphanic moment, Nate saw the big picture of Chatbooks: They had built too much. "Entrepreneurs need to drown out many voices along the journey, like naysayers or investors who reject you. But I had also shut out customer voices. I was too stubborn with my original vision," he explains. "It took those closest to me to see this blind spot." Nate decided to scrap their complicated product and start over.

His five-person team went on a two-week "Print-My-Instagram" sprint. While building the product, Nate tested the demand for this service on social channels. "I was immediately bombarded with requests like 'How do I get mine?!' and 'When will it be ready?'" he told me. "It was the clear signal I needed to keep going."

With their new product and positioning in place, customers flooded in. Their purpose and foundational story remained the same, but their evolutionary positioning—"Print Your Instagram"—tapped into a relevant social trend and connected with buyers succinctly. Chatbooks quickly ran out of capacity and had to hire teams of people to keep up with demand while building the infrastructure for scale.

Eight years later, Chatbooks made $50 million in profitable sales annually, becoming a monster in its category. Its positioning has since evolved beyond the original "Print Your Instagram" but remains grounded on its core promise: a "ridiculously easy way to share, print, and enjoy your family memories." Today, they sell products that allow customers to print photo books made on their smartphones and subscription services to print "monthbooks"—a play on yearbooks—for families. The company has become more than Nate ever thought possible.

As Nate put it, "Your story must connect with people on a

deep level . . . but also fit on a hat. If you don't have your story in three words, you don't have it yet."

The Story of Your Second Act

Many stuck companies are like Nate's in the early days, solving an apparent problem but in an overly complicated way that doesn't strike a chord with the buyer. Either they haven't found the right problem or the right story. This chapter assumes you've figured out the right problem to address after all the work in this book. Now is the time to let the market know how you will solve that problem for good. It's time to work on positioning.

Positioning is the story we tell about improving our customers' lives. It is the place your company occupies in the hearts and minds of your buyers. Excellent positioning excites people and de-positions competitors by putting them in the "old" box of mainstream companies that don't get the way the world is changing.

Excellent positioning creates mini-movements by telling evocative stories about the "new way" of doing things their products and companies are introducing. Airbnb: Find your home anywhere. SoulCycle: Exercise should be tribal. Warby Parker: Glasses can be hip and inexpensive. HubSpot: You can win customers with great content. Great stories are why these companies stood out—and their competitors didn't.

Great positioning is also more than a story. It is an encapsulation of your business strategy. The two are inseparable. If your core is the engine inside your car, your positioning is the body, with its sleek curves, colors, and road-ready features. You had a story before this point. It's impossible not to have some positioning. But now that you've transformed your business and corralled the resources to make it happen, you can start a bigger conversation with your market. It's time to craft the story of your second act.

The business world is like an art class in elementary school. Most kids color within the lines and draw cute pictures of dogs and houses. But there was always that one kid who drew a fire-breathing Pegasus riding a rainbow over skyscrapers to a candy castle in the clouds. That one drew people in when the drawings were hung up on the wall. Most kids don't learn the difference between creative confidence and arrogance, and "don't rock the boat" messaging gets programmed into their spirit.

In the business world, that reticence to stand out is still there. Companies try to please too many types of buyers or are too broad in their positioning (checking the box on all the features instead of telling a strong story). This is an opportunity to create your own fire-breathing Pegasus that stops people in their tracks. It's time for a bold story.

Just like parts of chapter 6 may be "old hat" for finance professionals, this chapter may cover known territory for marketing leaders. That said, I've tried to illuminate the unique elements of positioning for a company in its second act. But if you're comfortable running company positioning projects already, you can skim this chapter.

SAM LAWRENCE:
THE ART OF GREAT POSITIONING

Over the years, I've worked with Sam Lawrence on many projects. He was my CMO at Jive in the early days and helped me
with the Mobilize turnaround (chapter 6). He was also CMO at
Expanse, founder and CEO of Crushpath, an EVP at McCann, and
VP of marketing at CNet. One of the best business storytellers I
know, Sam can turn an IT security software company into a brand
as tight as Pepsi. He has taught many startup founders how to
tell a compelling story that addresses the company strategy and
customers' needs.

How do you think about positioning?

I imagine a company and its products like a tent in a sea of souks
within a loud and hyper-competitive bazaar. Like sellers, most
companies like to focus on basic marketing tactics like place-
ment (where you show up, "cornering the market"), the selection of
the products offered (how they're displayed and why), the reason
for the pricing (luxury? a steal? at parity with the rest?), and the
buying experience design (easy, hard, fun). But, they should consider their positioning: the story people tell about their souk (e.g.,
"everything handmade locally, the way it used to be!"). The virtual
world has made it much easier to take a spot in the bazaar but
much harder to see how competitive and noisy the overall market
is. More reason to truly understand the full scope of the marketplace and its sellers and to craft, control, and deliver your unique
market positioning within the appropriate section of that market.

What does it mean to have a strong position?

A strong position is a clear point of view and delivery plan that
drives every element of the business and its strategy. These

elements of positioning—your product, service, marketing, and other key parts of your go-to-market—add up to support a prevailing story, whether you've crafted it or your competitors have crafted it for you. The result is that people either think things like, *I don't get it*; *that's just a carrot peeler*, or *that the company believes tools should be super easy to hold.* A strong position is immediately evident in the product (e.g., "Check out the huge, soft grip on that carrot peeler!"). The clearer and more consistently evident the story, the more easily people can agree or disagree. Should kitchen tools have big silicone grips? Yes or no? Pro-life or pro-choice? Mac or PC?

Why is positioning important when building a breakaway company?

If a company is unnoticed within the bazaar of souks, it could shutter tomorrow, and no one would care. A breakaway company needs a strong position to survive. Most startups lack resources, so breaking away can't cost a ton. They can't erect a giant flashing sign or start selling self-flying planes. But stories are free to engineer—that's the good news. The bad news is that because stories are free, people think they are easy to craft and anyone can do it. Positioning is often passed to the marketing team and considered no more than a tagline change, which is the equivalent of believing you can put an ice cream label on a box of broken glass. Positioning isn't a slogan or campaign; it's how everything is delivered. Coming up with a good one is f-ing hard. Positioning must be led by the CEO, who oversees how it's delivered across all parts of the company.

How do you create the narrative?

First, step back from the company and clarify your category. You'd be surprised how unclear this often is—especially for breakaway

continued

companies. Be sure to use simple category language that buyers are already familiar with. Once you identify your category, ensure everyone in your team agrees on it—is it eggs, accounting software, or thermostats? To re-frame a narrative, attach a "novel" prefix to your existing category—things like "smart," "electric," "gluten-free," or just "free." How would that change your market position and delivery? What would it take to make that idea real? Do you have the right team, resources, and timing to deliver it? Creating a new narrative is its own book, but this is an easy way to start iterating on some meaningful directions.

How do you get it out to the world?
You don't. If the story is strong enough, customers and prospects get it out to the world. You must be laser-focused, clear, and consistent on how the positioning is delivered and ensure the product or service does the talking for you. If buyers open some fancy ice cream packaging to find broken glass, that story will get out to the world.

What Is Positioning?

Positioning distills the essence of your strategy into bite-sized elements that guide your company's decisions—from product design to pricing to customer interactions—and creates a deep connection with your customers.

Search Google for "great positioning," however, and you'll get a list of stock stories of famous brands or basic advice about how to build a positioning statement (e.g., "We build X product for Y customers and are different because of Z."). But these run-of-the-mill positioning statements barely scratch the surface of what good positioning can be: a powerful narrative that pulls people into its orbit because it transcends the dull market into something special. It is the difference between "we fix these very specific problems" and "we are the future of this industry," between being another player in a crowded market or emerging as a category-defining behemoth. Excellent positioning is a breath of fresh air blowing into a stagnant market, compelling buyers to learn more.

Great positioning should reflect your company's purpose, values, mission, and strategy—captured in your one-page plan (see chapter 4). But most importantly, it should capture your worldview: that critical insight, gained through extensive experience in the field, about the "broken" state of the market and how your company will improve your customers' lives. For example, Chipotle observed the increasing backlash against unhealthy ingredients at chains like Taco Bell and found a way to improve lives by using quality ingredients. Their site expresses their worldview: "Chipotle was born of the radical belief that there is a connection between how food is raised and prepared, and how it tastes." That insight drives the company's strategy, positioning, and organizational design down to how food is served.

When most people think about great positioning, they think about Nike. Nike started with a core niche: less expensive, lighter-weight shoes for runners (initially just track runners). The company saw great success in the early days and expanded into many adjacent shoe categories. But by the early eighties, the competition became fierce and Nike couldn't rely on innovative shoes as the means to grow. Instead, they put energy into their story: motivating people to push themselves athletically. That worldview—and the positioning that encapsulated it—was immortalized with the "Just Do It" campaign and the company's mission "to bring inspiration and innovation" to every athlete globally. And as far as Nike is concerned, if you have a body, you're an athlete. This positioning changed the game and allowed Nike to expand into myriad categories.

Strong positioning not only encapsulates your values and strategy but does it in a way that connects deeply with buyers. While you don't need *all* of the following characteristics, here is a list of aspirational qualities that should guide your thinking:

- **Relevant:** Your story connects to a significant global trend you are educating your market about. It must suggest where the future is headed and that you represent the change your market needs.

- **Emotional:** Your story strikes a chord with your ideal customers. It shouldn't just explain how your company makes money (e.g., "we sell shoes to X"); it should also evoke a higher purpose and tug at people's emotions. In the shoe industry, a retailer's positioning might evoke fun (Zappos), empathy (Tom's Shoes), self-confidence (Bruno Magli), or even social consciousness (Rothys).

- **Smart:** Ideally, your story describes a worldview—your worldview—that is obvious and brilliant, like a great movie with a surprise ending that makes complete sense upon reflection (e.g., *The Sixth Sense, The Usual Suspects*). For example, Halo Top making low-calorie ice cream that tastes good.

- **Compassionate:** Your story should focus on those you serve. Even if you're selling semiconductors, your story should connect to people's needs, desires, or pain points. That's what Howard Shultz, CEO of Starbucks, did when he said, "We're not a coffee company serving people; we're a people company serving coffee."

- **Competence:** Your story should convey that you are the best at what you do. Doing so balances the emotional side of your story: You are doing something big and inspiring and you are excellent at it, too.

- **Resonant:** Your story should position you as a "breath of fresh air" in an industry that needs it. When JetBlue appealed to leisure travelers (over business travelers) with seemingly obvious perks like gourmet snacks and more legroom, travelers felt heard.

- **Focused:** Your story should claim your part of the market and define it well, whether you are building a new category or disrupting an existing one. Consider how payments company Stripe focused on developers as their audience instead of trying to "swim upstream" and sell to executives in large companies.

- **Simple:** Your story should be succinct. Ideally, a version could be told in three words (e.g., "Print Your

Instagram"). This allows it to spread quickly and to start a conversation with attention-challenged buyers.

Patagonia's positioning exemplifies these elements coming together in a narrative. The company appeals to consumers who care about environmental concerns (relevant, emotional, simple) with well-designed, life-long products focused on the outdoor gear market where Patagonia can be the best (smart, confident, focused) and with a buying and return process that feels uniquely human (compassionate, resonant). This positioning, the company's strategy made simple, has turned this company into a beacon of what companies should do in the future—serve not just employees, customers, and owners but the planet. "Earth is now our only shareholder" is displayed prominently across their site.

If you've defined your core well (see chapter 3), you have the foundation of your positioning. You know your "best in the world" strengths and uniqueness, which likely harkens back to the founding of the company (or "refounding" if the company's core has gone through a significant transformation) while setting the stage for your future. Turning these raw materials into the right story can look simple upon reflection but take a long time to create. To craft a great positioning, you need to:

1. Gather the elements of your story: Pull together the raw materials that will form the basis of your positioning, such as competitor sites, former positioning from earlier phases of the company, and industry trends.

2. Define your category strategy: Decide whether to play in an existing category or create a new one and how that might change over time.

3. Create your point of view (POV): Craft the "manifesto" of your positioning—how you will change your buyers' lives for good.

4. Draft your positioning: Complete all your company's narrative elements to start the conversation with your market.

Start by assembling the right positioning team. I like to pull together a three- to five-person crew that includes the CEO, the head of marketing, outside advisors, or other team members with a penchant for storytelling. Pick a leader for the team and be clear about each member's roles and how decisions will be made. Once that's in place, you can start collecting the raw materials for your positioning.

1. GATHER THE ELEMENTS OF YOUR STORY

Screenwriters don't usually sit down and start writing a screenplay. Usually, they play the role of architect first: They generate high-level outlines, plot points, character arcs, scene descriptions, key conflicts, and tension points on 3×5 cards stuck on a corkboard (or the digital equivalent) and play around with those elements until they feel the story is tight. Only when all the pieces fit together do they feel ready to draft the screenplay.

Positioning is similar. You can't just jump in and create your narrative without seeing the bigger picture of how all the elements come together. You must answer strategic and market questions and collect the elements that will congeal into the right story. Many of these have likely been answered in your work throughout this book but now need to be considered in terms of the underlying story.

Start with the following questions, and as you come up with key answers, ideas, or insights that are relevant to your position, write them down on Post-it notes or a digital whiteboard:

- **How has the world changed?** What are the massive, undeniable trends that are affecting your customers? What is broken today, and how is it changing? What forces are shaping the landscape? Examples could be generational shifts (e.g., younger generations taking over the workplace), technology shifts (e.g., an increase in corporate use of AI), or shifts in cultural values (e.g., mental health becoming a bigger priority).

- **What have other players missed?** Look at your competitors' websites. Take screenshots of their home pages and paste them onto a presentation. What themes and patterns emerge? Are they all telling similar stories? How do they each see themselves as unique? What common language and core ideas do they rely on? Are they addressing a long list of problems instead of positioning around a strong core idea? What larger pain point are they missing that might be an opportunity?

- **What do your buyers genuinely want?** Customers don't always know what they want. Like your competitors, they may instinctively think about your product only regarding its tactical features. Your role is to dig deeper into their frustrations and aspirations to uncover what they want and need. For instance, a company that sells software to financial controllers might realize that its competitors are touting their products' ease of use. But a closer examination of these buyers might uncover that most want to become CFOs. Instead of focusing on features, the financial software company's positioning could tap into its customers' career aspirations: "Our software puts you in the driver's seat of financial planning and the path to CFO."

- **What positioning have you used in the past, and what did you learn from it?** Was there a consistent theme to your old narratives? Or did you try lots of stories? Ask customers, sales reps, or industry experts what worked and what didn't. Perhaps there's a seed of your new positioning in the remains of your old stories. If you "refresh" your story rather than start one from scratch, ensure the revised story has the elements of a great positioning described earlier in the chapter.

- **How are you uniquely suited to drive a better future?** Why you? Are your team, IP, and business model the best suited to deliver on your worldview? How is your core related to your chosen strategy? Can you back up your strategy and positioning with legitimate claims and investments? If not, what do you need to become the best?

- **How would you want an outsider to tell your story?** Imagine someone at a party telling another partygoer about your company. What would you want them to say? Why would the person hearing about your company care? Can you find a narrative that outsiders love to share because it makes them feel in the know (e.g., "I'm obsessed with this new luggage—it's like Apple created a suitcase")?

The results of this exercise should be a collection of trends, market insights, customer needs, and company strengths that will help you map out the basis of your positioning. However, before you can do that, you need to dive deeply into one uniquely important element of your positioning: your category.

2. DEFINE YOUR CATEGORY STRATEGY

The business world likes to put companies into buckets or "categories" that encapsulate what companies do, whether developing software, publishing books, or manufacturing hair care products. These categories and their lines of delineation are constantly shifting—and when they do, they can make or break companies (and their competitors). Determining how you fit into buyer categories is a huge part of the positioning process. Will you play in an existing category and disrupt it from within? Or create a new category and disrupt the market from the outside?

Playing in an Existing Category

Entering or further committing to an existing category means you'll face more competition, but the market for the product is known and predictable and buyers are already spending money on those products. You likely have a sense of the winners and losers and the opportunities for disruption. How to play a category to your benefit, however, will depend on that category's maturity. An existing category is typically in one of these three phases of maturity:

Phase 1—Emergent: When the category is new, players attack from all angles. The space is not clearly defined yet. To win in this category, you need a strong worldview, including an understanding of the technology and innovations that will drive the category forward, a thesis on how players will likely come together (future mergers), and a sense of the timeframe of how the category will mature. Get input from analysts, customers, prospects, and competitors on where the category is headed around which you can build your story.

Phase 2—Maturing: When a category is maturing, buyers are familiar with the offerings, but a clear leader hasn't been established. Your best strategy to win in a maturing category is to be the catalyst that pulls "all the pieces together" and creates a complete solution in the buyer's eyes. Your story should capture the market's imagination by thinking big about product development, partnerships, mergers and acquisitions, or other defining moves. Become the clear, visionary leader by painting a picture that brings the disparate pieces together before any other player.

Phase 3—Established: When a category is established, it has been defined by one dominant player. To win in this stage, follow the leader but find a meaningful differentiator that the category leader can't replicate. That becomes the anchor of your positioning in the overall category or a smaller subcategory. That could mean establishing a market niche (e.g., how FedEx created the category of express mail), a new model (e.g., how Netflix beat Blockbuster by mailing DVDs), or a revolutionary feature (e.g., how Zillow's Zestimate feature, which showed homeowners what their house was worth, drove the service's popularity). Also, watch for the tail end of an established category's lifespan, which happens around 10 years after one big idea has reshaped that category. As a category begins to wind down, that can signal the start of an emergent category.

If you go after an existing category, having a strong worldview that guides your strategy and positioning is vital. Whether your positioning focuses on product, design, business model, or another innovation, it must tap into a needed market shift and make clear how you will drive that shift.

Creating a New Category

Creating a new category around your offering is difficult but can pay off in spades if well executed. And it's a fun ride. Companies that successfully create new categories typically see higher valuations and faster growth than those that play in an existing category. Uber, which took business away from an existing category (taxis) and built a new one (ride-sharing), or White Claw, which took business away from the beer and wine category with a healthier alternative ("LaCroix with alcohol"), are great examples. Here are a few of the signs that it may be the right time to create a new category:

- **Few companies are telling a similar story.** Ideally, you are the first mover in this new space with a unique offering that sets you up to win. But it's only when the competition joins you in this new movement that the market takes off, and the press and analysts recognize it as a category. In other words, you don't want to be the only player for too long; you want to be the one that sets the tone for everyone in the category—like Airbnb does for the home-sharing category while its main competitor, Vrbo, mostly follows along as the clear No. 2.

- **Early adopters are ready for something new.** When you pitch your story to potential customers, do they vehemently agree with the idea? Is it clear that you're on to something huge, and you can execute on it? Many people you talk to will tell you what you want to hear and be nice about what they think of your idea. You want people to take out their wallets and beg you to participate in the beta process or become an early customer. You'll know you're on to something when you get a "Please, I need it now!" response.

- **You can deliver on the value proposition profitably.** Be honest about what you can build, sell, and support. It's easy to develop unique ideas and get people excited about them with designs or presentations. It's another thing to build it and take it to market profitably. Be ambitious but realistic. If your story is too far removed from your ability to deliver, you're not ready to build a category yet.

- **You can pull people from alternative offerings.** In the B2B world (and often in the B2C world), to create a new category, you must bring in dollars that would have gone to another category. For example, if you're offering a new funds transfer service for small businesses, can you convince customers to move away from traditional banks? Is there a 10X improvement for them to do so? If not, why will they make the switch?

- **There is an analog from another industry that lights the way.** If companies in other sectors with similar innovations have created a new category, that's a good sign. Learn everything you can about the strengths and weaknesses of their approach so you can amend your position as necessary. What can be learned from those markets? What made that innovation successful that could be replicated?

- **Your competitors are taking the same old approach.**
  If your competition is tightly bound to old, industry-accepted strategies, there is an opportunity for a new category. Like in judo, you can use your enemy's momentum against them. Creating a new category could counter your competitors' narratives in an undefendable way. Consider Salesforce going up against Siebel and other CRM players in the late nineties and early 2000s: Salesforce embraced the Cloud as its business model, while its competitors couldn't move to the Cloud without rebuilding their business operations from scratch.

In addition to starting a new category from the ground up, you may want to consider these options as the means to building a new category:

- **Combine separate categories into a new category.** An example of this would be a merger of two companies that sell to the same buyer but support adjacent customer needs. If one company sells *supply* forecasting software to manufacturing organizations and another sells *demand* forecasting software, they might merge to create a new category of holistic manufacturing intelligence.

- **Start in an existing category and shift customers to a new one over time.** If the world isn't ready for your "big idea," or you are not prepared to execute it properly, consider joining an existing market with enough differentiation to win business. Then, use that market to build your new category. At Jive, for example, we played in the "collaboration software" space for many years before building our own category around "social business software." Playing in an existing category gave us the time and space to be patient. We were able to capitalize on a huge trend (Facebook) when it came around and become the leader of a new category with a real business behind us.

Whatever you decide, make sure you think deeply about your category strategy. I'm always surprised by how deeply embedded categories are in buyers' minds and how much impact they can have during a company's growth phase. And once you have that strategy in mind, you can start developing your story, starting with your POV.

3. CREATE YOUR POINT OF VIEW (POV)

With steps 1 and 2 completed, you can now create the foundation of your positioning: the POV statement. The POV turns the materials you gathered earlier into a concise, inspiring narrative that supports the other positioning elements. It's intended to "start the conversation" with buyers and answer these questions:

1. What significant change is affecting your market?

2. What opportunity does this change represent?

3. Who is your company, and what is your unique offering?

4. What have your competitors missed?

5. Is there an analog from another industry that paves the way for what you do?

6. How will your service transform customers' lives for the better?

Your POV may change as trends and strategies shift, but doing it well shows your market that you have strategic clarity. Often, the narrative is hardened with success when you have "cracked the code" on the market. Here's an early, rough version of a POV I did for Mobilize, which you may recall from chapter 6 was a company that sold community software to membership organizations. Most of these organizations used our software like a private LinkedIn for their members with networking and professional growth, so we doubled down on that differentiator.

> Your members don't want to be sliced and diced. They don't want to be put into segments, funnels, and pipelines. But your organization is stuck with a "rearview mirror" of historical data and no sense of what customers are trying to accomplish, where they're headed, or how they want to grow. This blind spot misses a big opportunity—a new way to connect, not based on campaigns or artificial intelligence, but on what customers and prospects want: professional connection, opportunities, and growth.
>
> It's time for Professional Growth Networks (PGNs)

from Mobilize. LinkedIn showed the world the power of professional networks. Now, we bring that power to membership organizations through secure, exclusive communities for meaningful business connections.

PGNs provide deep insights into an organization's customers while creating an impenetrable moat of loyalty that drives dominance in your industry. PGNs are a marketplace of opportunities, jobs, initiatives, training, and events, all based on where your target customers want to go, not where they've been. That's how engagement turns into outcomes and how communities become movements. It's time to connect, not with ad-driven networks or generic community software, but with authenticity, purpose, and belonging. It's time to Mobilize.

How do you draft a POV? Here's a process I have seen work well:

1. **Draft the POV elements with a small team.** Brainstorm the core ideas that will drive an inspiring POV. Avoid using past examples and start from scratch. Take good notes, find agreement on the core principles, and then have the best writer in the group take a stab at a few drafts. Fine-tune it with the team until you're happy with the result.

2. **Test the draft with team members.** Share your draft with employees. Does it resonate? Does it excite them?

Redraft as needed, then go "outside the building" to advisors, board members, or other experts close to the company. Ensure it's clear, stirring, tight, and ambitious—but realistic.

3. **Test the polished version with the market:** This part of the process might be combined with the section on Investigating Breakaway Strategies from chapter 5 (page 129), where you get feedback on potential strategic directions. Or, if you've already decided on your new strategy, the POV ensures you can pull in customers with the story of that strategy. You can send them the text of your POV or review it in person to get feedback. Do the ideas land? Do customers nod vigorously in agreement? Or do they have trouble understanding? You want them jumping out of their chair and yelling, "Yes, that's it! It's about time!"

Real-world responses to your POV determine if it's on target. Does it come off as unique, inspiring, and powerful? Can it guide your team's decision-making? Does it align with your purpose and values? Does it give you enough wiggle room to evolve your strategy over time? Is it too aspirational that it stretches credibility? Or is it so tactical that it fails to inspire? Ideally, your story is visionary but backed up by what you can do today.

The most potent brand narratives elicit strong responses—positive or negative. Having people disagree with your position isn't necessarily bad, as it starts a conversation. Some of the strongest narratives are polarizing. Trying to please everyone is a surefire way to be unseen. Don't fear being unliked; fear being invisible. A strong reaction may indicate that a shift is happening, and people are on both sides. You want to be on the side of progress.

A POV is the most comprehensive of the positioning elements, so completing it will allow you to move on to the final step.

4. DRAFT YOUR POSITIONING

The following collection of positioning elements will guide your company's messaging: website content, sales scripts, advertising copy, internal communications, customer segmentation, and email footers. Your marketing team will have a clear direction, and your employees will be excited. But most importantly, your customers see you as the industry's future.

Each element of your positioning has a unique purpose, outlined below. I've also included an example of each element from my time at Mobilize.

Tagline

What is it? Your tagline is the two- to five-word synthesis of your positioning, encapsulating your brand and its values in one pithy phrase. This is your version of "Print Your Instagram" or "Just Do It." Ideally, it doesn't change frequently and strongly connects with your customers.

Why do you need it? A strong tagline will showcase your brand and story to customers in one quick moment. It's the start of the conversation—a meaningful opening salvo that drives people to learn more.

Mobilize Example: Communities Just Got Professional

Value Proposition

What is it? While the POV showcases your overall vision, your value proposition is a tight, externally facing summary of the problem you solve, the results you drive, and how you are unique. It should also de-position your competitors. I like to have a three- to six-word headline (what you might see on the company's homepage) and a fleshed-out description that supports that headline.

Why do you need it? A strong value prop is a sign of a strong strategy. It is the difference between winning and losing a sale, between a website visitor starting a chat session with you or moving on to a competitor.

Mobilize Example: *Professional communities that turn prospects into members and members into lifetime devotees.*

Positioning Statement

What is it? The positioning statement is an internal document that describes what you sell, to whom you sell it, and why you're the best option. The standard format is along the lines of:

"We make [insert product] for [insert target market] who are struggling with [insert pain point], and we are unique from other players in the [insert category] because of [insert differentiation], which drives [insert benefit]."

I also include a clause about where the company is headed, depending on where you are in your transformation, as a further point of differentiation. Something like, ". . . and our investment into [insert upcoming innovation]."

Why do you need it? Unlike the value proposition, the positioning statement is an internally focused element that ensures everyone on your team understands the strategy at a high level and that business decisions are aligned with your brand.

Mobilize Example*: "We provide community software and services for mid to large professional organizations who are struggling to engage members, and we are unique from other players because of a data-driven outreach system, an outcomes-focused services team, and our investment into future features for deep user profiling and analysis, all of which drives increased sales, conversion rates, retention, and differentiation for our customers."*

Brand Descriptors

What is it? This is a list of the words you want to be associated with your brand—not the SEO keywords, but the adjectives that should define the company, such as competent, fun, bold, accessible, innovative, secure, or flexible. You might have three essential descriptors along with a longer "supplemental" list that provides a more complete understanding.

Why do you need it? This maintains a consistent personality across departments and customer touchpoints.

Mobilize *Example*: <u>*Essential*</u>: *Thoughtful, Consultative, Tech-forward.* <u>*Supplemental*</u>: *Friendly, Empathetic, Genuine, Professional, Empowering, Collaborative, Data-Driven, Considerate, Diligent, Curious, Passionate.*

Note: I haven't included examples for these next two elements as they are lengthy and can vary across company types.

Personas

What is it? Personas represent your target customers. You may have one or 10, depending on your buying segments. For each persona, describe who they are, their goals, needs, pain points, and desires.

Why do you need it? Personas clarify and humanize your marketing efforts by determining what messages to deliver to whom and through which channels. They strengthen your ability to understand your buyers' perspectives and treat them accordingly.

Company History

What is it? Your company history is a bite-sized version of how your company got to where you are today, told in an inspiring, authentic way. Assuming a good story (and there almost always is), your history will be an inspiring way to tell people who you are, how you got here, and why you're doing this.

Why do you need it? Your history humanizes your company. It is another angle on your positioning that should feel authentic and inspiring to readers.

An Opportunity to Stand Out

I recently joined a sales call where the prospective customer referred to the competition—a large PE-owned business—as "they who shall not be named." He was so incensed with their level of service and hard-edged approach to dealing with customers that he said he would never support them again.

Like so many companies being managed solely focused on future exits, this competitor had missed the opportunity to serve customers in a way that created differentiation. The pressure to perform in the short term goes against the grain of creative positioning.

But when your business is lean, focused, and profitable, surrounded by a great team and supportive board, the stage is set for your company to emerge as a visionary leader in whatever category it decides to play. You are not hamstrung by unrealistic growth expectations that water down your story in pursuit of quarterly numbers. You can be bold. You can be patient. You can go big when the time is right.

Finding the right positioning is a colossal step in your company's transformation. It signifies that you have completed your transformation and have the right strategy, and your market is responding. The revenue might take a while to materialize from your positioning, but it will happen if you run the process well.

Congratulations on getting to the end of the process. Having been through this journey multiple times, I know it is fraught with challenges. Getting to the point where you can tell your reinvigorated story to the market is huge. It's a chance to get a bird's eye view of what you and your team have accomplished and the brighter path ahead for you and your customers. This is a time to reflect and celebrate. You've earned it.

Hard Lessons

In 2010, I joined the board of directors of a software company after it had raised an A round from a notable venture firm. While the company was very early in its journey, it was closing deals and had carved out a nice niche in its category. A year later, they raised a B round from another great firm.

After raising this much money on a relatively small business—and sensing the pressure to "triple, triple, double, double, double, go public" (i.e., 3X growth for two years and 2X increase in the three following years, followed by a public offering)—the CEO and founders were starting to pull their hair out. They were struggling with how to pull off that growth in their niche.

Instead of doubling down on the core business it had worked so hard to build, the team frantically sought new strategies to find growth. Instead of sharing information about the market experiments they were conducting with a small group of employees while they tested them out, they told a new story to the whole team and market every time they tested a new strategy, which seemed to be every six months.

Customers, board members, partners, and media were confused. The product team couldn't keep up with the changes needed to support each new positioning effort. Many deals the sales team closed were akin to consulting contracts rather than software licensing agreements, as the company had to build custom software to support the various new customers with each positioning shift.

Eventually, they ran out of money and the company was sold for pennies on the dollar, not having the revenue, IP, or market traction to justify much value.

As a board member, I failed them. I could have shined a light on the mistakes. While their core was not in a sexy, high-growth space, it was a strong starting point for future growth. The positioning was strong. However, their growth experiments should have been done in a bounded, safe way with a small team, separate from the core business. Only when you find the vein that will drive needed growth should you commit to a new story and shout it from the mountaintops.

Telling your story to the world, in other words, should be the final step of your positioning work and your overall transformation process. It should happen only after you've taken your stuck company through a deep and thoughtful shift into a lean, focused, purposeful organization capable of bringing needed change to your market.

Then and only then is it time to celebrate. Seeing how the market responds—not only to the new company you now represent but to the hard work and dedication it took to get to this point—is profoundly rewarding and worthy of reflecting upon.

Give Yourself to the Process

Achieving a more conscious participation
in a richer story proves a great gift after all.

—**JAMES HOLLIS,** *What Matters Most:*
Living a More Considered Life

The company I helped found in 2001 and discussed
at the beginning of the book, Jive Software, went
public on the NASDAQ at 9:30 a.m. on December
7, 2011. Board members, investors, executives, and some
handpicked employees enjoyed a glitzy morning: pictures in
front of the building with our ticker symbol on the jumbo-
tron, ringing the bell, brunch, and cake with our logo. We
mingled, sipped champagne, and nibbled on catered food—a
jamboree of capitalism.

It was a time to recognize what we had built, starting as a tiny, bootstrapped company only a mile from the NASDAQ building. I was no longer involved in the company, having stepped down as CEO and chairman a year earlier to be with my family, who barely saw me during the company's ramp to IPO. I was grateful for sharing the company's beautiful journey to IPO with some wonderful people, but something didn't feel right.

We had reached the most significant milestone of entrepreneurial success: taking your company public—at a time when it was rare to go public. I had "made it," according to how society and the media define success for entrepreneurs. But I didn't feel different. I felt worse. After the ceremony, I left. I had no idea where I was going. I strolled from Central Park to Christmas Elmo in Midtown to the holiday skaters at Rockefeller Center to the dive bars of the East Village. I walked all day like a meandering, urban Forrest Gump, brooding and pondering.

It was not my company anymore, so why was I still feeling this way? Despite the outward success of Jive, I felt like a disease was spreading behind the shiny veneer of the IPO and company marketing—an engine of perception management masking deeper problems. I couldn't let it go. And I felt responsible for what it had become.

From its IPO in 2011 until 2017, I watched the company I helped found and led for nine years die a slow, painful death on the public markets. It was like sending your straight-A kid to college only to watch her drop out to play hacky sack professionally. The company shifted its energy from innovation to financial outcomes, bending over backward to hit financial targets in an increasingly competitive environment. Differentiation waned as the company did anything to win deals. Growth fell below the magic 30 percent number for public companies, and the stock price tanked. In the end, Jive sold for a fraction of its earlier value to a PE firm of last resort. Once a raging source of purpose, community, and soul for me and many others, this company had been transformed into a slave to quarterly numbers that it failed to hit and became a loser.

I watched this drama play out from the outside. I scratched my head at what went wrong. We had turned a free software tool for online discussions into a juggernaut over nine years. First, we ran it profitably with no funding and built a massively valuable company; then we raised money to grow aggressively and failed; then we got cash flow positive again and crushed it; then the company raised a massive amount of money and slowly died. When we were lean, we were awesome. When we pushed too hard, we blew it.

In the following years, thanks to all manner of therapy, workshops, retreats, meditation work, dharma talks, and psychological deep dives, I began to understand my role in Jive's demise. Instead of pointing fingers at the board and execs who came in, I recognized how I had set the destructive wheels in motion. I set the wrong goals. I brought on the wrong investors, board members, and execs. I operated from a compromised position instead of a place of enlightened leadership.

Why? I was insecure. Surrounded by entrepreneurs, executives, and a business community that encouraged raising capital to succeed on a larger scale, I made decisions that would look good to investors or peers—or that they were telling me to make—instead of considering the long-term health of the business. Instead of building a unique, customer-first business, I followed a growth "playbook." As we scaled, I surrounded myself with a playbook team that saw the company as a vehicle for wealth creation rather than an opportunity to build something meaningful. I was fearful of looking bad. The system exploited this fear to motivate me and push an aggressive and unstable growth agenda.

My fierce desire to win drove decisions that ultimately killed the company. More importantly, I was doomed to repeat this pattern unless I dealt with its root cause. At first, this awareness was painful as I replayed the domino chain of decisions that took the company on its ruinous path. But it was ultimately freeing to see how it could have been different. If nothing else, I could use my experience at Jive to help others avoid similar situations. It was exciting. I felt like I had cracked a code. That's why chapter 2 was so important for me to include.

In working with hundreds of companies, I've seen what it looks like to get unstuck. Not all companies can be saved, of course. Sometimes, the market doesn't provide the needed receptivity for growth. Sometimes, the team burns out. Sometimes, a new entrant crushes your dreams. But many companies can be saved if the right elements are in place. Beyond smart people and operational excellence, several factors are unique to successful transformation. I hope this book provided a clear sense of what these are, especially the importance of having the right people, a strong core, and a thoughtful growth strategy.

But above all, you need a transformation mindset. Success is the goal, but an unbridled obsession to win can blind you to the truth. Having a transformation mindset includes understanding what drives you and how to optimize for the purpose and motivation in a long, selfless path to redemption. It also means embracing austerity and finding the excitement in how much can be done with a small, committed team. It means killing your ego and showing up to serve. You may already have had this mindset before you did the work I recommend in this book, but it's always worthwhile to check in and recommit to becoming what the company truly needs. The company won't transform until you do.

Ultimately, your role is to be a steward for a group of connected people on a mission. You are there for the ethical, responsible organization of resources toward the creation of value across all stakeholders: customers, employees, shareholders, and society at large. Transformation is a chance to recommit to building your business the right way and ensuring everyone's lives are made better in the process.

You may need to build a new product from scratch. You may need to save the company multiple times before it emerges from the dark of stuck-ness into the light of sustainable growth. Startups rarely follow a consistent path, and the transformation journey is just as unique to the company as its product. But I can guarantee if you commit to the work in a healthy, responsible, committed way, the people involved will be grateful.

Even if it wasn't in the cards for the company to make it, the growth, connection, and ultimately, the love everyone involved feels for each other, and which they will bring to whatever they do next, will be worth it.

The ultimate freedom comes in letting go of self and committing to the work.

Good luck.

Self-Assessment

Chapter 1

This chapter should prompt deep thinking about the state of your company and what led to its issues. Hopefully, you now know whether a transformation is possible. And if it is, hopefully, you have more conviction in executing that journey. To deepen your understanding of your situation and your conviction, consider these questions before moving on to the next chapter about the mindset that led to your current situation.

1. What elicited the most potent emotional response when you read about the five primary ways companies go astray (hiring the wrong team, fixating on revenue over strategy, losing focus, buying into a distorted narrative, or failing to manage through disruptive shifts)? Which of those five issues got your brain firing or resonated most with you on what happened or how you could fix it?

2. What systems can you and your team implement to

periodically evaluate your company's five most common problem points?

3. Think about your founding members, your team, and your investors. Who would be most helpful in evaluating the challenges and devising a path forward?

4. If you could change one thing in your company's history, what would it be? What decision do you regret the most? Would other team members agree, or is that issue more personal to you?

5. How do you feel after reading the chapter? Are you more convinced you can turn things around? Or did it bring up fundamental issues that might prevent a transformation?

Chapter 2

This chapter is meant to illuminate any mindset issues behind getting stuck. It is essential to evaluate the energy you and your team brought to the company in the past and to shift whatever patterns and mindsets no longer serve the organization. As you contemplate the ideal leadership style and approach for the transformation, consider these questions:

1. Did any stories (Jessie at Ampush, Kirby Winfield, Raj Kapoor at FitMob) resonate strongly? Why?

2. Think about your core motivation(s) for starting and leading your company. Are those motivations still

driving your decisions, or has fear taken over? If it's fear, how can you reorient your focus to infuse your passion into the company?

3. What is the one thing you would change in the next era of the company (and for your career)? What shift in mindset would dramatically improve your leadership abilities?

4. What realistic, actionable goals can you set to move out of whatever negative mindset you are stuck in? How can you work on those goals daily?

5. Beyond the individual perspective, is there a collective mindset for the company that needs to change? How will you implement that change?

Chapter 3

This chapter is about reconnecting with your core business. Often, companies get stuck trying to expand too quickly beyond their core and waste time, energy, and money in pursuit of fast growth. Regardless of whether that happened for your business, focusing on your core is critical to long-term health. These questions may help you clarify your core:

1. Before getting stuck, did you and your team discuss your core business and have a shared understanding of it? Looking back, which of the ideal characteristics for a core business (clear, defensible, and leads easily into other markets) was the weakest?

2. What members or groups can you involve in determining your core? Who would best aid you in reestablishing the fundamental elements?

3. If you created a core business "map" for your company, what initiatives would be farthest from your core? Can you easily move away from these things, or would they require a complete overhaul?

4. If you returned to the company's start and founded it again, how would you describe the business you are building to outsiders? Employees? Customers?

5. What activities and principles will you implement to protect your core moving forward? How will you know when investments are straying too far from your core?

Chapter 4

This chapter is about galvanizing your team around the company's next phase. This is the time to establish a new world order and correct the mistakes of the past. It's also a time to put aggressive growth goals aside in favor of a robust and stable operating model. To ensure you are putting the right "constitution" in place for this phase, consider the following questions:

1. Where were employees the most confused or frustrated in the past? Which teams or departments were furthest away from the goals of the business? How can you correct that misalignment?

2. Looking back at your old strategy documents and company goals, what did you get wrong? Were you too aggressive, unfocused, or erratic (inconsistent), or were there other reasons the goals were off?

3. How can you connect with your team daily? How can you make them feel included during the restructuring process?

4. How would you want your employees to describe your mission (five- to ten-year goal) in one sentence? What about your strategy (how you will win)?

5. Identify the areas in your business that are most volatile. What steps can you take to move towards stabilizing those areas?

Chapter 5

This chapter is about finding growth opportunities once the business is stable enough to focus on them. If you successfully organized around your core, you can seek growth that stems from that core. But it requires thoughtful analysis before putting meaningful investment behind it. To decide if you're ready, consider these questions:

1. Think about successful businesses that inspire you. What were their breakaway moves? Is there a similar "chess move" you could make?

2. What is your biggest fear when it comes to expansion?

Might previous missteps hinder your ability to find a breakaway move?

3. Sometimes, we shift from overly aggressive to overly conservative when we experience failure. Are there experiences that might make the company too "gun-shy" with growth? How can you overcome that fear?

4. When you scan your competitors' home pages and contrast that with buyers' pain points and desires, what is the big "missing?" Besides features and functions, is there an energetic missing or market blind spot that would excite potential buyers?

5. Like DocSend did with "Project Couch Change," how could you distill your growth strategies into achievable, bite-sized efforts that lead in the right direction but don't break the bank getting there?

Chapter 6

This chapter is about financing your growth intelligently once you have a solid plan. Warren Buffett famously said, "Risk comes from not knowing what you're doing." Once you know your core and have conviction in your growth plan that stems from that core (assuming you plan to grow), how can you finance the plan without taking on too much dilution or increasing the risk of failure? These questions may help you get started:

1. Which level of growth plan outlined in the chapter (stay

the course, expand cautiously, or grow quickly) does your company currently fall under? What factors or parts of the business led you to place it in that category?

2. If you were to create a growth plan dashboard for the company today, how would you answer the four questions outlined in the "3. Measure Your Progress" section on page 169? How would those answers change based on where your business is now versus where you want it to be?

3. Is your entire executive team behind your growth plan? If not, what are people's biggest fears with the plan? Where is your head, heart, and gut on the growth plan? Do you have a strong conviction in your ability to execute?

4. What would your growth plan look like if you didn't raise more money? How would that plan create shareholder value (less growth but less dilution)?

5. Are there old investors or board members who are no longer aligned with the new path of the business and are hindering its ability to execute? If so, how might you elegantly transition them out as part of an investment round or restructuring?

Chapter 7

This chapter illustrates the power of positioning, especially after a company's transformation. Once you have conviction in your new path, you can build a compelling narrative around it that pulls people into your orbit. The challenge is finding the right story that is innovative and inspiring but not so far removed from your current offering that it falls flat. To find the right positioning, consider these questions:

1. Like the Chatbooks case study, if you were forced to tell your company's story to the market in only three words, what would they be? Could you develop ten versions and test them with your team?

2. What beliefs surrounding your strategy are most deeply held by you and your team? What could you do for customers that would electrify your team?

3. What category do you think your business best fits in? What category disruption strategy would create the most value? Is that a viable strategy?

4. What do you imagine the categories will look like in five years? Ten years? If there was one winner in your desired category ten years from now, what would they have done well to get to that position?

5. Using the elements from the "Draft Your Positioning" section, brainstorm what each of these would look like for your company. Do they fit within your core? Would you feel confident bringing these ideas to your other team members?

Index

Index

Index

Index

About the Author

DAVE HERSH is an entrepreneur, investor, coach, and advisor based in San Francisco with over 30 years of experience in business strategy and startups. His ideas on building lean, profitable, human-first businesses have helped hundreds of businesses get "unstuck" and find their breakaway path. He is currently a general partner at Metamorph Capital, which acquires venture-backed companies in need of restructuring and transforms them into healthy, sustainable leaders. Dave was the Founding CEO of Jive (NASD: JIVE), which he grew from a small open-source project to its IPO in 2011. He then spent two years as a Board Partner (investor) at the VC firm Andreessen Horowitz.